David Tacey is Associate Professor of English and Reader in Psychoanalytic Studies at La Trobe University, Melbourne. He is the author of eight books on psycho-analysis and cultural studies, including *Jung and the New Age* and *The Spirituality Revolution* and co-editor (with Ann Casement) of *The Idea of the Numinous: Contemporary Jungian and Psychoanalytic Perspectives*.

HOW TO READ

Available now

Forthcoming

HOW
TO
READ

JUNG

DAVID TACEY

Granta Books

London

Granta Publications, 2/3 Hanover Yard, Noel Road, London N1 8BE

First published in Great Britain by Granta Books 2006

Extracts used with kind permission: 'An Eipstle from Holoferne's' (1960) in
Selected Poems by Sydney, Angus and Robertson, 1992. By arrangement with
the Estate of A. D. Hope c/o Curtis Brown (Aust) Pty Ltd. *Memories,
Reflections and Dreams*, 1961, reprinted by permission of HarperCollins
Publishers Ltd © C. G. Jung; *The Collected Works Of C. G. Jung* by C. G.
Jung © Routledge, reprinted by permission of Taylor & Francis Books UK.

A CIP catalogue record for this book is available from the British Library.

1 3 5 7 9 10 8 6 4 2

ISBN-13: 978-1-86207-726-3
ISBN-10: 1-86207-726-6

Typeset by M Rules

Printed and bound in Great Britain by
Bookmarque Limited, Croydon, Surrey

CONTENTS

SERIES EDITOR'S FOREWORD

How am I to read *How to Read*?

This series is based on a very simple, but novel idea. Most beginners' guides to great thinkers and writers offer either potted biography or condensed summaries of their major works, or perhaps even both. *How to Read*, by contrast, brings the reader face-to-face with the writing itself in the company of an expert guide. Its starting point is that in order to get close to what a writer is all about, you have to get close to the words they actually use and be shown how to read those words.

Every book in the series is in a way a masterclass in reading. Each author has selected ten or so short extracts from a writer's work and looks at them in detail as a way of revealing their central ideas and thereby opening doors onto a whole world of thought. Sometimes these extracts are arranged chronologically to give a sense of a thinker's development over time, sometimes not. The books are not merely compilations of a thinker's most famous passages, their 'greatest hits', but rather they offer a series of clues or keys that will enable readers to go on and make discoveries of their own. In addition to the texts and readings, each book provides a short biographical chronology and suggestions for further reading,

Internet resources, and so on. The books in the *How to Read* series don't claim to tell you all you need to know about Freud, Nietzsche and Darwin, or indeed Shakespeare and the Marquis de Sade, but they do offer the best starting point for further exploration.

Unlike the available second-hand versions of the minds that have shaped our intellectual, cultural, religious, political and scientific landscape, *How to Read* offers a refreshing set of first-hand encounters with those minds. Our hope is that these books will, by turn, instruct, intrigue, embolden, encourage and delight.

Simon Critchley
New School for Social Research, New York

ACKNOWLEDGEMENTS

In writing this book, I consulted several colleagues and fellow scholars about matters of definition and argument. These include Ann Casement, John Dourley, Don Fredericksen, Lucy Huskinson, Andrew Samuels and Murray Stein. My sincere thanks are due to these colleagues for their support at various stages in the writing of this work. I would also like to thank my editor, Bella Shand, for her insightful suggestions and creative attention to detail. However, I must accept responsibility for what goes to print in this work.

I would like to record my debt to two mentors and recent masters of the field, Edward Edinger and James Hillman, who have helped to translate and update Jung's insights for the contemporary world.

INTRODUCTION

Jung is an enigmatic figure in the history of modern thought. For almost a hundred years his works have inspired many people and been a source of insight to intellectuals, artists, practitioners and general readers. He has opened up doorways to the psyche, to the mystery of life and to spiritual meaning. He has awoken several generations to the power of symbols, to the ancient world of myths and the healing capacity of dreams. Jung has brought the possibility of enchantment and spiritual depth to a post-religious Western society which has been living without a shared spiritual story or cosmology for some time.

In his lifetime, his work was beset by controversy, and historians of psychology have often been unable to evaluate his achievement. Science in his day seemed almost embarrassed by his writing, as he spoke about the influence of gods or *archetypes* (structural forms or motifs of the psyche) on behaviour in an era of rationality and measurement. His work has been attacked as unscientific, mystical and speculative. In his defence, Jung claimed his science was a 'depth psychology' that looked beyond the surface, whereas academic psychology looked only at what was rationally explicable. Jung's work may appear less scientific to some readers, due to the relative absence of detailed case histories in his writings. Jung tended to write in a philosophical style, providing his findings and conclusions rather than the empirical facts upon which such conclusions were based. He seemed impatient with details, and keen to articulate a big picture.

Jung was larger than any single discipline and went in pursuit of truth outside the normal boundaries. His concern was not only with psychiatry in its clinical application, but with life in its broadest possible meaning. He went in search of many aspects of the psyche and the world in his quest for understanding. The title of one of his mid-career books, *Modern Man in Search of a Soul* (1933), reflects the breadth of his vision. Because he had the courage to tackle big issues, Jung always enjoyed a popular following. Many in the wider community felt that Jung was speaking to their emotional and spiritual needs, and was not merely addressing a handful of colleagues in the medical profession.

Jung set himself the task not only of acquiring new knowledge about human personality but of breaking through to a level of wisdom where knowledge generally stops. His major questions included: Are we related to something infinite or not? Do forces beyond reason impact on our bodies, minds and behaviour? Is meaning inherent in existence or is it added by ourselves? Are gods real or do we merely invent them?

These questions seemed oddly unscientific to many in Jung's time. They are the perennial questions of philosophy, and yet medical science had narrowed itself to an experimental and clinical base in which the broader issues played no part in human health. Jung was looking for spirit in an age of science, and his day did not respond kindly to his longing. Our time has more sympathy for him, because we live in a postmodern era in which many of the assumptions of science and modernity have been questioned, doubted or reversed. Our age is hungry for meaning, and Jung speaks directly to this post-rational or post-enlightenment hunger.[1]

Jung was researching the unconscious for several years before he met Freud. He had developed the word association test (which indicated how speech patterns are affected by unconscious problems), introduced the idea of the *complex* (split-off psychic fragments with a semi-autonomous existence), studied psychopathology (the science of mental disorders) with Pierre Janet in Paris, and researched schizophrenia with Eugen Bleuler in his native Zurich. Freud's work interested Jung because the psychological origins of mental disease were being explored, and Jung felt this would throw light on the unknown reaches of the mind.

Freud welcomed Jung's interest because Jung was highly intelligent, strongly motivated, and able to advance the cause of psychoanalysis beyond Jewish Vienna to the psychiatric world and to the Christian West, where Freud was keen to make inroads. 'Jung's association with us,' Freud wrote to Karl Abraham in 1908, 'is the more valuable for [through him] analysis escaped the danger of becoming a Jewish national affair.'[2] Freud anointed Jung as his 'successor and crown prince',[3] but no sooner had Freud announced his intentions than Jung began to express discontent with the Freudian point of view.

Jung found Freud's views to be confined to the same materialistic assumptions that he had encountered in psychiatry. Even as early as 1908, Jung had become critical of what he called Freud's 'dogma' of infantile sexuality, his insistence that all symptoms be traced to childhood traumas, his strict adherence to the Oedipus complex, and his formulaic approach to dream symbolism, where everything seemed to symbolize a penis or a vagina. Nor did Jung agree with Freud's model of the psyche with superego, ego and id. For Jung, these were arbitrary and simplistic categories which did not adequately describe the landscape of the psyche.

Freud was moving into deep areas but, according to Jung, with a narrowness that prevented him from understanding much of what he saw. Jung wanted everything in psycho-analysis to be open-ended, to be receptive to the possibility that forces governing the future and not just the past had a role to play in the personality. Jung called for a wider conception of *libido* or energy, a more symbolic approach to dreams, and recognition of a forward-striving movement in the psyche. Freud seemed to want to link everything back to early childhood; Jung sought to show that the psyche was urging us onward to create a new and broader personality.

All of these elements frustrated Freud. He did not want Jung to turn the psyche into a poetic or literary field in which vague philosophical principles would govern what happens in the mind. Jung, a symbolic thinker with a background in German romantic and Greek philosophical traditions, was attracted to big ideas and mythological forces or archetypes that could never be explained in rational terms. Jung argued that the archetypes were 'given' with life, and had to be accepted as the foundational structures of life. This sounded to Freud more like mysticism than pure science.

Jung's father was a clergyman, his mother was spiritual in the folk or popular sense, and his family tree was grounded in the soil of religious thinking. Although Jung had rejected the practices of his father's Swiss Reformed Church, he remained committed to the life of the spirit, and felt cramped by Freud's approach, which found a rational cause for every problem. Jung rejected Freud's conception of the unconscious, arguing that the mind is not merely personal but has a universal and religious dimension.

The archetypes, which he defined as universal forms of the collective unconscious, did not originate from personal experience, but from a Platonic realm of ancestral ideas and memories. In many ways, Jung is the intellectual descendant of Plato, who postulated an ideal realm of abstract forms (invisible metaphysical constructs), whereas Freud is the heir of Aristotle, who strove to understand the world through reason and logic.

Jung's concepts were not fully developed during his collaboration with Freud (1906–13), but Freud saw them in their early, nascent form, and he had seen enough. To Freud, Jung seemed to be abandoning science for magical thinking. He saw Jung replacing the scepticism of the scientific attitude with affirmations about religion, cosmology and philosophy. In a sense, Freud was right, and I sympathize with his anguish. Jung was intuiting a level of psychic reality that was not 'scientific' in the normal sense, and Freud had to either abandon science and follow Jung's lead, or abandon Jung and stick to science as he knew it. He chose the latter course.

Jung was a religious philosopher with scientific concerns; never, in my opinion, a pure scientist. Jung hoped that others would join him in his quest, but most scientific colleagues closed ranks. If he would not respect scientific boundaries, nor would those who upheld those boundaries show respect for him.

In 1913 the British Medical Association set up a 'committee' for investigating psychoanalysis with Ernest Jones (a major figure in the Freudian school) at its head, and part of its brief was to disestablish Jung and discredit his work. This committee seems to have been successful, and its impact is still felt today. Negative associations to Jung and his work have stuck in the minds of professionals, so that when anything Jungian is raised in conferences or discussion papers, medical people tend to think of these elements as unorthodox, unscientific or unfounded.

The break between Freud and Jung was probably inevitable. What was startling was that two such widely divergent thinkers, one governed by suspicion, the other by affirmation, could have maintained their close association for the time they did. Both must have had their doubts about the other, but in their mutual interests they suppressed them. Freud must have seen very early that Jung was a visionary thinker. Jung must have realized that Freud was committed to science and would not tolerate departures from it. Jung had hoped that a hunger for truth would assert itself in Freud, and Freud hoped that Jung would come to his senses and drop his religious obsessions. Eventually, the hopes and dreams of both men collapsed, and they had to accept the unadorned reality of their differences.

But Western civilization is all the poorer for this split. We now have to renegotiate the divorce between science and religion, empiricism and philosophy. In Jung's time, it was too early to bring about a reconciliation between these apparently opposite elements of mind. The future challenge within the field of psychoanalysis and indeed beyond is to heal this division, and when it does so, the opposition between religion and science will be overcome. Both Freud and Jung were great thinkers, yet Jung's greatness may only become clear in the future, because his work has relevance for a future task, which is to rediscover the totality of life, and not to be content with exploring fragments of it in specialist disciplines.

The break with Freud not only damaged Jung's professional

confidence and reputation, but it precipitated a near-psychotic upheaval from 1913 to 1919, which Jung describes in his memoir, *Memories, Dreams, Reflections* (1961). These years were teeming with fantasies, psychic eruptions and chaotic thoughts. He experienced instability, anxiety and premonitory intuitions. Any psychiatrist would recognize this as a mental breakdown, but Jungians like to refer to this period euphemistically as his 'confrontation with the unconscious', or as a 'shamanic illness' that preceded the birth of his new self, the mature Jung. There is no indignity, however, in the fact that an early healer of humanity's split psyche, and of the split between religion and science, should first have to heal his own broken soul.

To be called a 'prophet' or a 'mystic' can be a term of abuse, and Freud used this to great effect against Jung. Ultimately our response to Jung depends on whether we regard the task of linking science and religion as a worthwhile project. If we agree that it is worthwhile, we think highly of Jung and respect his role in the history of ideas. If we assume that fusing science and religion is a waste of time, we tend to have a low opinion of Jung and his work.

Jung sought to paint the psyche in rich and colourful hues, to reveal its depth, to expose its divine and daemonic reaches. In order to give it substance he borrowed from ancient religions such concepts as soul, spirit, anima, animus, although these terms had been obsolete for centuries. Above all, he mythologized the psyche as the contemporary site for religious experience. Whereas his father, Paul, had seen religion 'out there' in history, holy lands, scripture, ritual and tradition, Carl Jung wanted to see religion 'in here', in the cosmic forces of the psyche, in the interplay of psychic opposites, in dreams and visions, in the structures of mind that become visible in art, imagination, myth, literature and symbolism.

This was Jung's myth for modernity, offering it something to believe in. God was not dead but had changed his name and location. Salvation had become individuation, the spiritual art of becoming a whole person.

As science advances, it is becoming more open to the mystical possibilities of form, matter, time and space. Changes in physics, mathematics, chemistry, biology, medicine and psychology appear to be moving in Jung's direction.[4] Postmodern science has seen through the ideology of rationality and is more receptive to the mysterious, the holistic, the speculative and the universal.[5] Jung's archetypes and collective unconscious no longer appear as bizarre as they once did. The postmodern turn is a move away from reductionism to more speculative models where science and religion can be imagined as compatible, or as co-existent.

Jung was not wrong, just ahead of his time. As the hunger of the world shifts from gathering information to the search for wisdom, his works will emerge from the margins and play a more decisive role in shaping consciousness and culture. The postmodern era is above all a time when the 'margins' come into visibility, when centre and margin are likely to change places.[6]

1

THE LANGUAGE OF SYMBOLS AND DREAMS

We produce symbols unconsciously and spontaneously in our dreams. For instance, a patient of mine dreamed of a drunken, dishevelled, vulgar woman called his 'wife' (though in reality his wife was totally different). The dream statement, therefore, is shocking and utterly unlike reality, yet that is what the dream says. Naturally such a statement is not acceptable and is immediately dismissed as dream nonsense. If you let the patient associate freely to the dream, he will most likely try to get away as far as possible from such a shocking thought in order to end up with one of his staple complexes, but you will have learned nothing about the meaning of this particular dream. What is the unconscious trying to convey by such an obviously untrue statement?

Clearly, the dream is seeking to express the idea of a degenerate female who is closely connected with the dreamer. This idea is projected upon his wife, where the statement becomes untrue. What does it refer to, then?

Subtler minds in the Middle Ages already knew that every man 'carries Eve, his wife, hidden in his body'. It is this feminine element in every man (based on the minority of females genes in his biological make-up) which I have called the *anima*. 'She' consists essentially in a certain inferior kind of relatedness to the surroundings and particularly to women, which is kept carefully concealed from others as well as from oneself. A man's visible personality may seem quite normal, while his anima side is sometimes in a deplorable state. This was the case with our dreamer: his female side was not nice. Applied to his anima, the dream-statement hits the nail on the head when it says: you are behaving like a degenerate female. It hits him hard as indeed it should. One should not, however, understand such a dream as evidence for the *moral nature* of the unconscious. It is merely an attempt to balance the lopsidedness of the conscious mind, which had believed the fiction that one was a perfect gentleman throughout.

Such experiences taught me to mistrust free association. I no longer followed associations that led far afield and away from the manifest dream-statement. I concentrated rather on the actual dream-text as the thing which was intended by the unconscious, and I began to circumambulate the dream itself, never letting it out of my sight, or as one turns an unknown object round and round in one's hands to absorb every detail of it. ('Symbols and the Interpretation of Dreams', *CW* 18: 418-430)[7]

Jung believed that symbols are created spontaneously by the psyche. Our dreams are constituted entirely of *symbols*, which Jung differentiated from *signs*. Signs include names, emblems or images that point to something known. For instance, the name 'wife' is a sign that points to a known person, to this man's marriage partner. But symbols operate on a different plane, and point to something as yet unknown. The 'wife' in a dream points to an interior, psychic reality that does not correspond with outer reality. For Jung, the same word can function as a sign or a symbol, depending on whether or not it is being used by the unconscious to point to internal realities.

A sign is obvious, manifest and can be understood by reason. A symbol, however, is mysterious and can only be discerned by intuition or poetic understanding. It is symbolic knowledge that Jung is concerned with, and he is attracted to what is deep, profound and obscure. The study of signs leads to semiotics, linguistics and discourse analysis. The study of symbols leads to mythology, religion and philosophy. For Jung, the unconscious is not speaking about the external social world, but about the internal psychic plane, which cannot be known directly. It is *real* in its own right, though not in the sense that we usually designate as real, and symbols are the nearest we can get to approaching this unknown realm.

Dreams such as that of Jung's patient are disconcerting and confronting, since they tell the dreamer what he does not want to know about himself. It tells him there is another self inside his personality, and this self is undeveloped, vulgar and not respectable. In other words, it is a disturbing presence, and runs contrary to the social *persona*, which is adjusted to reality and presents as a gentleman.

Jung identified the 'wife' in the dream as the *anima*, which he understood to be the feminine and least developed part of the man's personality. Because this part is unconscious, it is projected upon women and external figures. The man does not know that he is *also* the anima, that he manifests this personality in himself, and is controlled and influenced by 'her' moods, judgements and needs. In the mythic language of the

Middle Ages, the male person 'carries Eve, his wife, hidden in his body'. This may seem implausible to reason, but Jung believed it is how the unconscious expresses the interior life of the male psyche.

The unconscious is like a parallel universe, peopled by interior selves and figures that correspond in part to the people of our day world, but who are by no means reducible to external realities. For Jung, dream selves are psychologically real, that is, they have emotional validity, and have to be treated as if they were persons. Our minds are conditioned to think that only what we can see and touch is real, but Jung questioned this view, and his psychology is a challenge to our understanding of reality. Jung was an unsettling thinker, because he introduced the notion that the evidence of our senses is illusory, and that common sense is nothing more than a construct of external conditioning.

Freud in comparison believed that dream images were residues or reflections of persons or events of our day world. He interpreted dreams and fantasies largely at the objective level, as referring to external things or processes. Jung saw this as a Western prejudice, and argued that we automatically (and wrongly) respond to dreams as reflections of external phenomena. To understand dreams, he argued, we need to postulate an interior reality, inhabited by internal persons, which he referred to as *archetypes*. The anima is one of the primary archetypes found mainly in the male psyche and the *animus* is another, found mainly in the psychology of women (see Chapter 6).

Unlike Freud, Jung interpreted dreams at the subjective level, as referring to internal objects and figures. Dreams are not comments on the day world, or censored versions of re-enacted childhood dramas, but are self-representations of an interior reality. If we can think in terms of *inner space*, peopled by symbolic figures and mythic forces, we have already begun to think like Jung. He referred to this as *introverted* thinking, whereas Freud's thinking was primarily *extraverted* and directed towards the external object or person. Although Freud explored internal reality, he did so with an extraverted gaze, often seeing the internal as a fantasy reflection of external objects. 'Introverted' and 'extraverted' are terms Jung invented partly to account for the differences in orientation between himself and Freud (*CW*6) and which have now entered everyday vocabulary.

To think like Jung requires effort and education, unless one is by nature an introverted intuitive, and then thinking like Jung is quite normal. Jung's patient, for instance, might wake up and think that the dream was a piece of nonsense. The drunken, dishevelled woman does not correspond to his wife in real life. He may feel that the dream is deceiving him and is a trick of the mind. However, if he can alter his perception, and see the woman as a symbol of an unknown aspect of himself, then he is thinking psychologically and therapeutically. As soon as this shift is made, according to Jung, we get on the dream's wavelength and begin to learn from it.

Jung's reference to free association in the extract is an attack on the Freudian method of dream interpretation, where the patient 'free associates' on the images and actions of the dream. To Jung, this approach was wrong because it takes us away from the content of the dream. 'Stick to the image!' he used to say to his students. The dream is a revelation from the psyche, and as such its meaning cannot be ascertained by activating the resources of personal memory or childhood history. It is a *transpersonal* message from the depths, and we should adopt a position of humility towards it. Jung believed the dream had to be approached with surprise and wonder, and we should be prepared for insights, both pleasant and unpleasant, that would be made known to us.

Jung's method of interpretation involves not association but *amplification*, a skill developed by the analyst in his or her clinical training. The object is to amplify the dream images by relating them to the myths and symbols of world religions, literatures and cosmologies. Instead of relating the dream to the personal history of the patient, Jung attempts to relate it to the universal history of humanity, to the symbolic systems that have enshrined wisdom in every time and culture.

For Jung, dreams are to the individual what myths are to civilization, namely, symbolic expressions of the spiritual or universal aspect of reality. Extraverted thinking tells us about history, events and people, but the intuitive and introverted thinking of the symbolic realm informs us of the universal forces that underlie our existence in time and space. There is no firm empirical basis for this belief in universal forces, but the intuitive traditions of literature, mythology and the arts are the main foundation for spiritual knowledge. Jung argued that personal dreams are more important today than ever before. In the past, Western man and woman had access to the universal symbols of the unconscious – the collective unconscious as Jung called it – through participation in myths and religions. We entered into the core of reality through ritual, ceremony, shared fantasy and story. But in our time, these reservoirs of meaning have dried up, as we have become more rational and intellectual.

The progress of humanity has been suspect, according to Jung, because we have amassed a lot of information but have little sense of the meaning of our lives:

We have become rich in knowledge, but poor in wisdom.
The centre of gravity of our interest has switched over to
the materialistic side, whereas the ancients preferred a
mode of thought nearer to the fantastic type. To the classi-
cal mind, everything was still saturated with mythology.
(*CW* 5: 23)

Our intellectual enlightenment has given us a great deal of
science about the world, but access to the universal layers of
meaning, found only in symbolic languages, has been radically
diminished. We tend to think of myths and religions as
'untrue', and of dreams as 'distortions' of reality. But for Jung
they are expressions of a truth that is truer than literal truth.

This is Jung's vital message, linking him to the 'perennial
philosophy' and to wisdom traditions that originate from
Heraclitus, Socrates and Plato. Socrates said truth is not self-
evident, and Jung would agree. What we see, and what we
seem, is not the whole truth. Our knowledge is not reliable;
it is partial and undermined by the fact that the unconscious
has a separate truth dimension, of which we are mostly obliv-
ious. Ironically, the deeper truth resides in what we habitually
dismiss as illusion, fantasy, myth and distortion. This may be
one reason why, in an age governed by science and logic, our
entertainment world is saturated with fantasy, mythic stories
and legends: a compensatory process has arisen in popular
culture.

The reason we have lost access to the deeper truth, for
Jung, is that we have lost access to the symbolic language that
discloses it. Our world-blinded consciousness has made a successful adaptation to external reality, but the cost has been an
atrophy of our symbolic life. Jung contrasts two modes of
knowledge, one governed by *logos* (the Greek word for reason

or science) and another governed by *mythos* (the Greek word for story or myth). Mythos knows the things of the world by personifying them. The forces of the psyche are experienced as 'persons' in a symbolic drama. These figures are felt to have subjectivity and intention, to have wills of their own, and to be 'gods' that control us.

The age of reason has seen the rise of logos and the demise of mythos. Jung was a counter-force to modernity in that he criticized logos and championed a return of mythos as a legitimate mode of knowing. Logos assumes that mythos was merely a bad or infantile version of science, a silly way of understanding the world. But Jung's defence of mythos was to argue that it is the best possible way of knowing the core of reality, that cannot be disclosed by science, logic or rationality. Jung believed the mythical mode of perception is not a primitive stage in the history of the mind, but a language in the structure of the mind. It is a language we lose contact with at our peril, because when severed from the symbolic domain we lose our relationship with the cosmos and with the deeper life within ourselves.

Jung modernized the mythical function by giving it new names. Instead of speaking of gods or demons, which sounded superstitious and obsolete, he spoke about the archetypes of the psyche, and the principal ones he called anima, animus, shadow, spirit, soul, Self, the mother, the father. In many respects these were the old gods of Greece and Rome revisited in a *psychological* form. Having these psychological versions of the old gods accepted by the scientific world was a difficult matter. Some felt Jung was regressing to the past, others that he was trying to invent a new religion. In championing mythos in a scientific age, Jung was in danger of being classified as an oddity, a throwback to ancient times, a mystic.

Jung was aware that his attempt to restore mythos as a mode of knowledge would meet with massive resistance, but he believed that the task of keeping in touch with the unconscious through the mythical mode was worth the risk of being dismissed as superstitious or irrational. In 1912 he published a major work *Symbols of Transformation*,[8] to differentiate his thinking from the materialism of mainstream science. In this work he argued to an astonished scientific public that the mind functions best when it is connected to archetypal symbols, which free us from the literalism of reason and link us to the regenerative forces of the psyche. In 'Two Kinds of Thinking' (*CW* 5: 4–46) he claimed that the use of reason to the exclusion of myth and fantasy makes us sick, because it alienates us from the sources of healing, which are only ever expressed in symbolic language. We have to recover the primordial mode of mythos, the 'fantasy thinking of the ancients', so that we can reconnect our lives with cosmic forces.

For Jung, health is synonymous with the overcoming of the ego's alienation,[9] and only a symbolic language can convey to the ego that it is already connected to forces that it cannot see or understand. The importance of art, Jung believed, is to give form to the things unknown, and the function of religion, from the Latin *religio* ('to bind back to') is to reconnect us to the sustaining forces that the ego does not recognize. Jung's term *ego* is virtually identical to Freud's; it is the centre of our conscious identity and selfhood. However, for Jung, the task of the ego is to transform itself by integrating as many contents of the unconscious as possible, in which case it begins to function as an ancillary organ of the Self (see Chapter 4).

Jung's use of mythic terms in psychological science proved divisive and controversial in his time, and still in ours. One often hears the accusation that Jung is a fantasist, woolly-minded or not 'factual' enough. This criticism ignores the fact that the psychological forces of healing, according to Jung, cannot be known directly, as rational concepts, but only indirectly, as poetic symbols. Critics often read his archetypes as mechanical or solid entities, rather than as enabling fictions that help us approach the unconscious with a poetic sensibility. Jung pointed to this problem time and again:

> In describing the living processes of the psyche I deliberately and consciously give preference to a dramatic, mythological way of thinking and speaking, because this is not only more expressive but also more exact than an abstract scientific terminology. (*CW* 9, 2: 25)

Jung recognized his terms were provisional and experimental, but they came close to psychic reality as he understood it. If the psychology of the unconscious departed from the symbolic mode, it would lose its ability to express this reality, hence: 'I do not wish or intend to give these intuitive concepts too specific a definition' (*CW* 9, 2: 29). Narrow definitions or rational terms would fail to grasp their meaning, and would also give the false impression that these psychic forms 'existed' in a tangible way.

Jung's archetypes were drawn from his clinical experience, dream research and studies in myth, culture and religion. The ego is the first archetype that we typically encounter, only we make the mistake of assuming it is the entirety of the personality. The *shadow* is close to Freud's alter ego, and represents all those traits, desires and contents that the ego has found unacceptable and has been forced to repress. In Jung's map of psychic development, the shadow is usually the second archetype that is encountered in the course of *individuation*, his term for personality development. The *anima* and *animus* personify the deep unconscious in men and women respectively, and more will be said about them in Chapter 6.

The *mother* and *father* are major personifications of the psyche, and are often found at the core of our complexes. They are shaped by our experiences of our real parents, but they develop separate existences of their own, and often have distinctly archaic or mythological features. The mother plays a major role in Jung's pantheon of characters, as she personifies the matrix of life, the origin from which the ego emerges, and to which it returns for the sake of rebirth and renewal. The ego often fears the mother, because it senses that it will be devoured in her embrace. Freud reads the return to the mother as a literal fantasy, and associates it with the desire for sexual cohabitation with the mother, an incestuous drive. For Jung, the problem is not incest as such, but the fear that the ego will not be able to free itself from the unconscious.

The father, for Jung, points to the realm of spirit and culture, and personifies law, order and meaning. If the mother is the deep unconscious, the father is the archetypal figure who acts as guarantor and sponsor of consciousness and spirit. Jung views the internal father as a mythological figure, and relates it directly to the image of God the Father in Western religion. But the father is also, for Jung, a personification of collective consciousness and moral conscience, and the individuating ego often has to battle to free itself from the iron grip of the father's moral law. At this level, the father is an obstacle to be negotiated as the ego makes its way towards individuation.

Jung never claimed that archetypes 'existed' in the sense that things of the visible world exist and have substance. To read Jung correctly, we have to understand his mythic mode of description and respond sympathetically. Inevitably, his mythic terms have been (mis)read as assertions of fact by the logical thinking of science, and many scientists have felt compelled to dismiss them out of hand as ludicrous.[10] Of course, they *become* ludicrous if we engage in this 'category error' and fail to grasp the subtle nature of their meaning. A certain slippage often takes place in the scientific reception of Jung: his *nonrational* terms and images are read literally – and not metaphorically – and they are made *irrational* by this process.

Historians and philosophers of science often engage in what they see as a heroic battle against Jung, to hold back the tides of his irrationality. The latest and most spectacular example of this is Richard Noll, an historian of science at Harvard University. Noll engages in an extremely literal reading of Jung's symbols and images, and seems to be deliberately misreading Jung to create a sensational result. In *The Jung Cult: Origins of a Charismatic Movement* and other works, he reads Jung as a charlatan and manipulator who conjures up illusions of spirits and gods to hoodwink others, and to establish himself as a new-age religious leader.[11] Noll's misreading of Jung has generated international controversy, and has activated a widespread anti-Jung feeling, especially in the scientific community. Jung scholars have responded to this crisis,[12] but it is difficult to assert the validity of his point of view while science fails to respect Jung's metaphorical language and symbolic thinking.

One way to reduce the damaging impact of this misreading of Jung is to break down the monolithic or static quality of his archetypal figures, and to treat them as *processes*, as verbs rather than as nouns. For instance, the ego or the shadow are not to be conceived as fixed and unchanging entities, but as fluid metaphors which point to a continuously changing psychic process. James Hillman achieves this perspective in his post-Jungian re-visioning of Jung's principles, and to some extent Hillman may be more palatable than Jung in the sceptical intellectual world.[13] Jungian thought can recover credibility if it rethinks its categories in terms of *movements of psyche* rather than as *objects*, which tempts sceptics to say, 'But they don't exist,' or 'It ain't necessarily so.'

Contrary to scientific prejudice, Jung did not *reify* his archetypes, that is, treat these metaphorical figures as concrete things. In relation to the anima archetype, for instance, he tells us that when a man is sufficiently familiar with the depths of his unconscious, the anima loses her personified and semi-autonomous character, and becomes instead a 'function of relationship' to the unconscious (*CW* 7: 370). In other words, the *figure* of the anima can, at the right moment, transform into a *process*. The autonomy of the psychic figure is dissolved, and the *dramatis personae* of the psyche are removed from the stage. Dreams and the imagination cease personifying the unconscious as a separate figure, and consciousness expands to include what had been invested in 'anima' as a part of its own psychic reality. This indicates that the autonomy of this figure was relative at the outset and that the psychic figures are imaginal, not literal 'persons'.

In moving from myth and religion to Jungian or analytical psychology we are moving from one mythic or fantasy system to another. For Jung, *fantasy* is not a derogatory term, but a discourse that most nearly approximates to the substance and movement of the unconscious. The aim of depth psychology is to *translate* the figures of the psyche from older, obsolete mythologies into new ones that have more conviction and perhaps come closer to our modern experience of the world.

We cannot escape myth or fantasy, but all we can do, Jung said, is 'dream the myth onward' (*CW* 9, 1: 76), in the hope that we can come to a better understanding of the mystery in which we are held. In this work of updating and translating, the role of the arts is crucial, as Jung realized (*CW* 15). Depth psychology, he believed, must work in tandem with the creative arts, whose task is to revive the ancient figures and forces by making them comprehensible to the modern imagination. Both the artist and the psychologist realize the necessity of 'making new' the ancient truths that have become opaque and obscure in our time. As the poet A. D. Hope wrote:

> Yet the myths will not fit us ready made.
> It is the meaning of the poet's trade
> To re-create the fables and revive
> In men the energies by which they live.[14]

2

THE SECOND SELF

Somewhere deep in the background I always knew that I was two persons. One was the son of my parents, who went to school and was less intelligent, attentive, hard-working, decent, and clean than many other boys. The other was grown up – old, in fact – sceptical, mistrustful, remote from the world of men, but close to nature, the earth, the sun, the moon, the weather, all living creatures, and above all close to the night, to dreams, and to whatever 'God' worked directly in him . . .

Besides . . . personality No. 1, the school boy of 1890 . . . there existed another realm, like a temple in which anyone who entered was transformed and suddenly overpowered by a vision of the whole cosmos, so that he could only marvel and admire, forgetful of himself. Here lived the 'Other', who knew God as a hidden, personal, and at the same time supra-personal secret. Here nothing separated man from God; indeed, it was as though the human mind looked down upon Creation simultaneously with God.

What I am here unfolding, sentence by sentence, is something I was then not conscious of in any particular way, though I sensed it with an overpowering premonition and intensity of feeling. At such times I *knew* I was worthy of myself, that I was my true self. As soon as I was alone, I could pass over into this state. I therefore sought the peace and solitude of this 'Other', personality No. 2.

The play and counterplay between personalities No. 1 and No. 2, which has run through my whole life, has nothing to do with a 'split' or dissociation in the ordinary medical sense. On the contrary, it is played out in every individual. In my life No. 2 has been of prime importance, and I have always tried to make room for anything that wanted to come to me from within. He is a typical figure, but he is perceived only by the very few. Most people's conscious understanding is not sufficient to realize that he is also what they are. (*Memories, Dreams, Reflections*: 61–2)[15]

Central to Jung's understanding of himself is that his *self* is plural. Someone with less imagination might say he or she had several *aspects* to the self, but Jung personified these aspects as separate selves. He argued against the assertion he might be schizophrenic with the qualification that: 'the play and counterplay between personalities No. 1 and No. 2 has nothing to do with a "split" or dissociation in the ordinary medical sense'.

The fact that Jung argued that this plurality 'is played out in every individual' does not remove it from the realm of madness, but makes it a common aspect of our experience. The question of madness arises when the plural selves get out of relation with one another, when they lose connection and become strongly opposed and contradictory. Then, we might say, neurosis, or more seriously, psychosis, is a real possibility.

Ironically, the more aware we are that we are composed of different selves, the less likely we are to suffer a full splitting of the personality. The plural self is 'normal' for Jung, and the aim of psychological health is to bring the diverse parts into living relationship, to act as host, as it were, to a harmonious community.

Jung reveals his second personality as old, wise and close to nature. He is a cosmic personality, and in psychological terms is a personification of the collective unconscious. The first personality, the young boy, is vulnerable and conscious of his failings, and yet this other self is universal, remote from society and close to eternity, God and night. The boy is located in a specific time and place, but the second self is outside these limits and in an eternal or archetypal realm. In theological terms, it is as if the ordinary ego is incarnated in time and space, but is connected to an eternal reality that is continuous with time, and intersects with time at moments of transparency or heightened awareness.

Many cultures have sensed this profound relationship between human and eternal realities, and have attempted to give expression to an intuition of 'heaven', and to significant cultural figures who have attempted to bridge the two worlds, such as Christ and Buddha. Jung speaks of 'passing over' into his true self, and leaving the world for the peace and solitude of this other personality. It should be noted that this second self is not to be confused with Jung's archetype called the Self (as discussed in Chapter 4). The Self is an archetype which expresses the totality of the psyche, and includes the ego and the unconscious, whereas Jung's second self is a personification of the unconscious only. In childhood Jung apprehended a deeper, older and more profound part of the human psyche that existed within.

'He is a typical figure, but he is perceived only by the very few.' These few, Jung argued, become 'wise', but everyone has a second self, at least potentially. When it is made conscious, people become creative. It is the second self, he believed, that generates creativity and intuition, whereas the ego – the first self – is more concerned with social adaptation and personal stability. The second self awakens us to new possibilities in ourselves and the world, and here Jung is talking about the age-old experience of *inspiration*, the sense of being inspired by a force that wells up from the unconscious and confronts the ego as an 'outside' influence.

We know from the history of art that the creative person is inclined to personify the source of inspiration as another person, a muse or inspiratrice. For instance, Dante attributed his creativity to Beatrice, Petrarch to Laura. In these cases, Jung would say the second self appears under the guise of the *anima*. The creative source of life is not always seen as human. Sometimes, for instance in indigenous cultures, it is experienced as a spirit, animal or bird which conveys messages to the receptive person. The personal burden is then to convert such messages into forms usable by society. They need to be written down, turned into art, philosophy, poetry, liturgy or moral truth.

What the creative person and the mad person have in common is that they are not confined to a single self located in the ego, but their subjectivity extends across a spectrum of possibilities. The mad person is diminished and overwhelmed by this diversity; the other selves invade the personality, creating havoc, dissociation and chaos. The psyche splits into several selves, such as are well known in psychosis and dementia. Madness is often accompanied by paranoia, a feeling that one is under attack by outside influences. This is because the

other selves are unconscious, and as such are projected out-
wards upon the world. The creative person, on the other
hand, is able to harness this sense of plurality, to work with it
and become conscious of it. If the right attitude is discovered,
this sense of otherness can lead to a rich flow of images, inspi-
rations and ideas, but only if the ego can cooperate and learn
to understand the interior process.

Jung felt his No. 2 personality linked him to nature, sea-
sons, elements, stars, dreams and the night side of life. This
was his enlarged or greater self, which in India is given the
term *Atman*, known as the God within. We in the West have
been forced by religious and social conditioning to forget or
ignore this larger self, but Jung argued it is intrinsic to human
nature and is found everywhere. Our civilization has failed to
encourage this greater self because we have been reduced to
the size of the ego, and the greater elements have been projected outside us upon God and the heavens.

Jung believed that when Christianity in its didactic, moralistic and non-mystical form is weakened by education and
disbelief, the greater self will be rediscovered, and will become
the key element in any new cosmology or spirituality (CW 10:
190). Christianity will not be destroyed, but will discover its
own mystical inheritance and help its followers converse with
the Christ figure within (CW 9, 2). His argument is that *gnosis*,
an ancient Greek term for knowing the God within, will
replace conventional belief in the God without. God, he felt,
transcends inside and outside, but our chief entrance to this
unfathomable reality will be through the inner life.

To live the larger unconscious second self is fraught with
problems. One is what Jung calls *inflation*, the enlargement of
the person to superhuman proportions. Such a distortion
causes arrogance, 'godlikeness', hubris and fantasies of mastery.

It is perhaps for good reason, he reflects, that Western religion has kept this greatness away from human reach, since only a highly sensitive and gifted person could realize that this spiritual self is not to be confused with the ego (the No. 1 personality), but represents a larger reality outside the ego. This self may be *within* us, but it does not *belong* to us. Rather, it springs from a divine source and is part of what Jung refers to as the *objective psyche*.

Jung assumes that this deep interiority participates in the God realm. For Jung, it is never a question of believing in God in the conventional sense; he says he knows this other realm within himself. A BBC interviewer, John Freeman, asked Jung if he believed in God, and he famously replied:

> Difficult to answer. I know. I don't need to believe. I know.[16]

In the same interview, Jung explained his difficulty with the notion of belief:

> The word 'belief' is a difficult thing for me. I don't *believe*. I must have a reason for a certain hypothesis. Either I *know* a thing, and then I know it – I don't need to believe it.

Jung speaks like a gnostic who claims to know God by virtue of his experience and personal knowledge. In Jung's ideal future, religious belief will be less important culturally, because people will pursue knowledge of God, and belief will diminish in stature. This position represents a peculiar mixture of the scientific attitude merged together with the mystical.

Jung describes in his memoirs how he struggled as a child to give expression to this second self. He tells how, in his tenth year, he took hold of a school ruler, and carved from it 'a little manikin about two inches long, with a frock coat, top hat, and shiny black books' (*MDR*: 36). He put this tiny figure in a pencil case, with a 'smooth, oblong blackish stone' that he had taken from the Rhine.

> This was his stone. All this was a great secret. I took the case to the forbidden attic at the top of the house and hid it with great satisfaction on one of the beams under the roof – for no one must ever see it! I knew that not a soul would ever find it there. No one could discover my secret and destroy it. I felt safe, and the tormenting sense of being at odds with myself was gone. This possession of a secret had a very powerful formative influence on my character; I consider it the essential factor of my boyhood. (*MDR*: 36–7)

All through Jung's life there was a fear that others might want to destroy his secret life, his second self, his sacred being. He felt that society, religion and science knew little about the second self, from which everything arises, and in which truth is found. At times it seems that Jung was paranoid about society's capacity to destroy his secret. Despite it being the essential nature of our being, people were opposed to the idea of the second self. Jung believed that the ego is threatened by the second self, and tries to defend against it by attacking it.

Jung was often plagued by fears of chaos and inundation, by threats of despair, and it was all the more important for him to fashion images of the second self that brought meaning and stability to the personality. He tells how he was led to create the manikin because of a sense of 'disunion with myself and uncertainty in the world at large' (*MDR*: 36). This symbolic act of creating a new self gave him 'a feeling of newly-won security' and the satisfaction that he 'possessed something that no one knew and no one could get at' (*MDR*: 37). By implication, we all need to fashion symbols of the second self, so we can transcend egotism and aspire to a security that the ordinary ego can never provide.

In religious terms, Jung had fallen out of Christianity and engaged instead with ancient religions where manikins, symbolic stones and tokens held enormous significance, were treated with the greatest respect and surrounded by taboo. He says that, in later life, the rounded pebble reminded him of the cache of soul-stones discovered at Arlesheim, Germany, and, further back, of the 'Australian churingas'. In Australian Aboriginal ceremonies of male initiation,[17] the young male is given a sacred stone or *churinga*, to symbolize the 'second body' or new life from which he must now live. At the climax of the ritual, the elder holds out the stone, and says:

Here is your body, here is your second self.[18]

There are parallels to this in all the world religions, where the profane and self-centred life of the ego is terminated, and a new self is put in its place. St Paul speaks to the Ephesians about 'putting on the new self that has been created in God's way' (Eph 4: 24). In tribal societies, the time for laying aside the old and putting on the new self is about the age of twelve or thirteen, when the boy is leaving childhood and finding a new basis for the adult personality.

In Jung's story, the second self is not passed to him by tradition or by an elder. His story is modern and outside tradition, and he invents a personal symbolism consisting of manikin, stone and hiding place. The modern person has ancient longings, so to speak, for the archetypal process of rebirth, but he or she has fallen out of tradition, and personal symbols and dreams become hugely important in the absence of a shared public symbolism. The creativity of the psyche must now take the burden of responsibility, and show the way towards rebirth and meaning.

We see in this childhood narrative several elements that were to become foundational to Jung's approach to psychotherapy. One is the importance of imagination and artistic expression to the inner life. Without imaginative expression, the inner life can be dulled, and never allowed to find its voice. Another point is the importance of ritual action to the well-being of the soul: the carving of the manikin, the hiding of it in the attic, the placing of scrolls of paper on which secret words had been written, are acts in which 'care of the soul' is being enacted. Thirdly, we see the importance of a secret as a way of affirming the reality of the soul. 'The little wooden figure with the stone was a first attempt, still unconscious and childish, to give shape to the secret' (MDR: 37). Ceremony, solemnity, secrecy – these must not be dismissed as esoterica, but are needed to help us transcend the mundane, and to give verticality and form to the spirit.

Living with the idea of a secret self is synonymous with isolation. In tribal societies, the secret of one's identity was given by elders and tradition. In modern society, the secret no longer inducts us into public ritual, but excludes us from the secular order. Jung believed it was important for people to have their secrets and not to yield to the pressure of conformity. A great many people, he argued, forfeit their secret self because they 'cannot bear this isolation':

> As a rule they end by surrendering their individual goal to their craving for collective conformity – a procedure which all the opinions, beliefs, and ideals of their environment encourage. Only a secret which the individual cannot betray – one which he fears to give away, or which he cannot formulate in words, and which therefore seems to belong to the category of crazy ideas – can prevent the otherwise inevitable retrogression. (*MDR*: 376–7)

He is saying that to have one's soul and be in the world at the same time, one needs to be a little crazy. The idea of an interior self is a 'crazy idea' to a world that seeks only material security and social adjustment. An element of craziness or eccentricity keeps us sane by dislodging us from an egocentric position, enabling us to maintain a relationship with the whole personality. A great deal of psychiatry advocates social adjustment at all costs, and Jung was opposed to any conditioning that leads to a betrayal of soul. He recommended that the values of society should be critiqued rather than replicated, and that we cultivate a little madness and some secret space, so that the soul can flourish.

3

THE UNDERGROUND GOD

The muted roar of the Rhine Falls was always audible, and all around lay a danger zone. People drowned, bodies were swept over the rocks. In the cemetery nearby, the sexton would dig a hole – heaps of brown, upturned earth. Black, solemn men in long frock coats with unusually tall hats and shiny black boots would bring a black box. My father would be there in his clerical gown, speaking in a resounding voice . . . Certain persons who had been around previously would suddenly no longer be there. Then I would hear that they had been buried, and that Lord Jesus had taken them to himself. Lord Jesus evidently 'took' reluctantly . . . but this 'taking' was the same as putting them in a hole in the ground.

This sinister analogy had unfortunate consequences. I began to distrust Lord Jesus. He lost the aspect of a big, comforting, benevolent bird and became associated with the gloomy black men in frock coats, top hats, and shiny black boots who busied themselves with the black box.

At about the same time . . . I had the earliest dream I can remember, a dream which was to preoccupy me all my life. I was then between three and four years old.

The vicarage stood quite alone near Laufen castle, and there was a big meadow stretching back from the sexton's farm. In the dream I was in this meadow. Suddenly I discovered a dark, rectangular, stone-lined hole in the ground. I had never seen it before. I ran forward curiously and peered down into it. Then I saw a stone stairway leading down. Hesitantly and fearfully, I descended . . . I saw before me in the dim light a rectangular chamber . . .The floor was laid with flagstones, and in the centre a red carpet ran from the entrance to a low platform.

On this platform stood a wonderfully rich golden throne. I am not certain, but perhaps a red cushion lay on the seat. It was a magnificent throne, a real king's throne in a fairy tale. Something was standing on it which I thought at first was a tree trunk twelve to fifteen feet high and about one and a half to two feet thick. It was a huge thing, reaching almost to the ceiling. But it was of a curious composition: it was made of skin and naked flesh, and on top there was something like a rounded head with no face and no hair. On the very top of the head was a single eye, gazing motionlessly upwards . . .

I was paralysed with terror. At that moment I heard from outside and above me my mother's voice. She called out, 'Yes, just look at him. That is the man-eater!' That intensified my terror still more, and I awoke sweating and scared to death.

The phallus of this dream seems to be a subterranean God 'not to be named', and such it remained throughout my youth, reappearing whenever anyone spoke too emphatically about Lord Jesus. Lord Jesus never became quite real for me, never quite acceptable, never quite lovable, for

again and again I would think of his underground counterpart, a frightful revelation which had been accorded me
without my seeking it. (*Memories, Dreams, Reflections*:
24–8)

All his life Jung was excited by the idea of God, and especially
by the possibility that our lives could achieve a connection
with an infinite reality. 'I find that all my thoughts circle
around God like the planets around the sun, and are as irre-
sistibly attracted to Him' (*MDR*: 13). His passion for God grew
stronger with age, so that his late memoirs are an extended
meditation on the experience of God.

But what God is Jung excited by? A theme in Jung's work
is that the conventional God is dead. In this sense, Jung was a
follower of Nietzsche, who proclaimed the death of God,[19]
and at first glance Jung seemed to support Nietzsche's atheism.

Jung believed that the God of religion was dead because we
had killed him with too much piety. We had made God shal-
low, narrow and good. This served to stifle and suppress the
vitality of God; the divine life had been depleted by too much
moralism. In other words, the desire to fashion God according to our highest moral ideals of perfection, has had a
debilitating impact on the divine image. The gap between our
religious image of God, and the incomprehensible reality of
God, has widened, causing the image to separate from reality,
to become emptied of meaning, and to collapse on account of
its artificiality and incredulity.

We have brought about the death of God because our religious imagination has been weak and unable to encompass
the majesty of the divine nature. Here Jung and Nietzsche are
in full agreement. We have reduced the divine to a moralistic
'man' in heaven, on a golden throne above the sky. This deity

has died, and yet God cannot die because God is immortal. Perhaps the *image* of God dies, while his life goes elsewhere, to await a rebirth. Jung's work argued that the dead God would be reborn from below, from the dark and womb-like chambers of the earth.[20] The God 'above' has collapsed, and the idea of God, Jung felt, will re-emerge from below, from the ground of the unconscious mind.

God in Jung's dream is 'buried' in the field which is adjacent to the cemetery of his father's church. God is funereal, motionless, terrifying, but nevertheless alive below the ground. The terror of the dream is emphasized by the fearful image of the 'single eye, gazing motionlessly upwards'. This appears to be a symbolic reference to the Eye of God (Zechariah 4: 10), an archetypal image associated with the terror of being closely observed by eternity itself. This God, however, 'sees' through the eye of its phallic head. We thought we had escaped the gaze and judgement of God, but he continues to watch us, as omniscient as ever.

The tomb of the old God's death is the womb of his rebirth. What the boy Jung witnessed in the dream was the rebirth of God in an antinomian vision in which convention is reversed in every detail: God (complete with golden throne) is not above the sky but below ground, not a 'man' but an erect phallus, not the stern judge of our sexuality but sexuality itself, not moralistic but wild and unpredictable.

Jung's father, Paul Jung, was a pious Christian minister who strove to keep alive his faith in a distant, remote, faraway God above the sky, but, according to his son, Paul's faith had died some time ago, largely as a result of the assault of science upon religion during the nineteenth century. The father tried to pass on his faith, but Jung could see that his father did not believe what he was preaching. Jung felt deeply for his father's plight and wanted to help, but he could not pass on his *own* faith to his father, because it was a different kind of faith. The son had been given a new image of God, a phallic, powerful, chthonic God who was emerging from the depths. This was a shattering and terrible secret for the boy, and Jung wrote, 'I did not say anything about the phallus dream until I was sixty-five. A strict taboo hung over all these matters' (*MDR*: 58).

It may seem incredible that a four-year-old boy should dream of a colossal phallus of this size and magnitude. Jung says he does not know 'where the anatomically correct phallus can have come from' (*MDR*: 28), although some commentators have speculated that it could be based on early sexual abuse from one of his eight pastor uncles, which Jung alludes to in his correspondence with Freud.[21] The scene is malevolent, and in the dream the boy shudders with fear, believing that 'it might at any moment crawl off the throne like a worm and creep towards me' (*MDR*: 27). His mother's cry that this is 'the man-eater' serves to intensify his terror.

Freudians might be tempted to suggest that this is a wish-fulfilment on the part of a growing boy. The glowing phallus might seem like a boy's dream of phallic potency and strength. This line of thought might be appropriate if he were, say, twelve or thirteen, but he is 'between three and four'. Freud or Klein, one of Freud's followers, might want to say that four-year-olds are not as innocent as we imagine. Be that as it may, Jung leaves aside the Freudian elements, and does not even entertain the hypothesis of early childhood exposure to sexual abuse.

Jung concentrates instead on the archetypal significance of this 'ritual phallus'. He thinks the dream sketches in the missing side of his childhood experience of divinity. His conscious thoughts about religion, encouraged by family, church and Sunday school, are felt to be unrealistic and one-sided. There is a missing side to the image of Jesus and God, and he argued that it is possible that 'the dark Lord Jesus [and] the phallus [are] identical' (MDR: 27).

The scandal of this association would be obvious to any religious person, who would insist that Jesus has nothing to do with a phallus standing on a throne, staring at the top of the stone chamber through its single phallic eye. More likely, a religious commentator would argue, this is a vision of the devil, and a sign that the boy Jung is dangerously close to the forces of evil. His wayward curiosity, his attraction to death, violent imagery and the 'dark side' has brought him close to the realm of pure, unregenerate evil.

Jung, however, did not believe that the dark subterranean figure was a pagan image of deity, a fallen angel or a vision of evil but was convinced that it was an aspect of God himself. This was a vision of God *after* the 'death of God'. It was God struggling to give new form and expression to himself. This was God reclaiming his otherness from the anthropomorphic images that had killed him, and being reborn in the instinctual realm. It never occurs to Jung the boy or man that this might be a revelation of evil. The mother's response in the dream suggests an internalized moralistic revulsion, but the effect of the dream is that Jung has been given a glimpse of something secret and sacred taking place within the divine itself. It is not a revolting but a revolutionary experience.

Jung sees this as a vision of growth, fecundity and dark vitality. The ritual phallus plays a huge role, for instance, in Indian art, where it symbolizes creativity and regeneration. It symbolizes the procreative side of the deity, its impregnating force and its capacity to give birth. The fact that this is occur-

ring underground, in a dark and ancient chamber, suggests
that the rebirth of the God has not yet reached general consciousness. Something is taking its course, but the collective is
unaware of it. A deity or king who is not acknowledged as
such is stirring below, while at the surface consciousness still
registers that God is dead and that we live in post-religious
times.

Jung emphasizes that the dream is a foreshadowing of his
exploration of new processes in the deep unconscious:

> Through this childhood dream I was initiated into the
> secrets of the earth. What happened then was a kind of
> burial in the earth, and many years were to pass before I
> came out again. Today I know that it happened in order to
> bring the greatest possible amount of light into the dark-
> ness. It was an initiation into the realm of darkness. My
> intellectual life had its unconscious beginnings at that
> time. (*MDR*: 30)

When the divine light is snuffed out by reason and logic,
we have to go into the darkness to discover what is being prepared. The prophetic imagination does not accept the
Godless condition at face value; it knows that a new chapter
is about to open in our relationship to ultimate value. Jung
says he was 'buried in the earth', a metaphor for being caught
up in the unconscious. The search for the divine would continue, although it could not assume the conventional forms of
religion.

Another psychic event of Jung's boyhood is illuminating here:
his daytime vision of God defecating on his own church. Jung
was leaving school one day and passing the cathedral in Basel
with its glittering, multicoloured roof, and he was 'overwhelmed

by the beauty of the sight and thought: "The world is beautiful and the church is beautiful, and God made all this and sits above it far away in the blue sky on a golden throne and . . .'". Here came, Jung recounts, 'a great hole' in his thoughts, and 'a choking sensation' (*MDR*: 52). Reluctant to think this vision through to its conclusion, Jung sought to suppress his thought for two days until, on the third night, he allowed himself to acknowledge the conclusion to the vision:

> God sits on His golden throne, high above the world – and from under the throne an enormous turd falls upon the sparkling new roof, shatters it, and breaks the walls of the cathedral asunder. (*MDR*: 56)

Jung describes his 'enormous, indescribable relief' at allowing this vision to enter his consciousness. 'Instead of the expected damnation, grace had come upon me, and with it an unutterable bliss such as I had never known. I wept for happiness and gratitude' (*MDR*: 56). Jung reflects:

> Why did God befoul His cathedral? That, for me, was a terrible thought. But then came the dim understanding that God could be something terrible. I had experienced a dark and terrible secret. It overshadowed my whole life, and I became deeply pensive. (MDR: 57)

We now have two terrible secrets: God as ritual phallus, and God's turd shattering the church. Through a conventional perspective, Jung appears as a blasphemer and blight on the religious life. In this vision we discern one of the major themes of his life: God and the church are not identical. God is frustrated with religion, and enraged at what it has done to him, expressed here in an aggressive act towards his own cathedral.

A psychoanalytic reading after Freud would find the anal aggressivity of the Oedipal son against his father's church, but this would ignore the archetypal dimension of the vision. The prophetic side of human experience can never be discerned if we reduce everything to personal dynamics. Jung comments that 'God refuses to abide by traditions, no matter how sacred' (MDR: 57). What is astonishing to many readers is that Jung never seems to question that he is of sound mind and not assailed by negative fantasies, and secondly, that it is in fact 'God' who is speaking to him in these unconventional ways. 'God had landed me in this fix without my willing it . . . and I was now certain that He was the author of this desperate problem' (MDR: 55).

If we apply conventional reasoning to Jung, he comes across as mad or obscene. But if we read his experiences as he reads them, we see 'God' involved in a drama of death and renewal. Jung does not accept that God has been fully revealed in the scriptures. Rather, he insists there is *ongoing* incarnation and *continuing* revelation. This is a gnostic view of God, and when the theologian Father Victor White of Oxford entered into dialogue with Jung, he was forced to conclude that Jung was outside the theological tradition and engaged in different perspectives on reality.

White's dialogue with Jung is partly traced in his book, *God and the Unconscious*.[22] White thought he had found a friend and colleague in Jung, and that they would together work towards a revival of Christianity. But as time went on, White began to fear that Jung was an antagonist of Christianity.[23] Jung does not accept the premises of theology, but sees the world through the lens of psychology, in which God is a metaphor for the fate and passion of ultimate meaning.

Victor White felt that Jung was saying God was 'evil' or had a demonic side. But Jung's view of God is similar to a Chinese philosopher's view of Tao. Ultimate reality is seen as an interplay of conflicting forces, *yin* and *yang*, darkness and light. Because Western religion has viewed God as yang and masculine (Father and Son), there has been a damning up of the energies that have been left out of the picture. With the collapse of the traditional image of God, the time is right for the release of yin aspects of the divine. These aspects include instinct, sexuality and the so-called 'dark side', and could never have emerged unless the official image had collapsed. Jung suggests that the breakdown of religion is inaugurated by God to allow a larger image of God to appear to the human imagination.

Jung's dreams and visions show the rebirth of God in the underworld, and the destruction of the old religious dispensation by a God who is above the moral code. His late works, *Answer to Job* and *Aion*, concern themselves with structural changes in the reformulation of the divine. In these and other writings, Jung shows why feminine aspects of the divine need to be incorporated into the image of the holy. Theologians tend to see blasphemy in his thoughts about God, but it could be that Jung is performing drastic surgery in an attempt to 'save' God from moribund religion, and to recover a prophetic imagination that has been long dead in the religious tradition.

4

MYTH, CONSCIOUSNESS AND THE STAGES OF LIFE

The psychic life of civilized man is full of problems; we cannot even think of it except in terms of problems. Our psychic processes are made up to a large extent of reflections, doubts, experiments, all of which are almost completely foreign to the unconscious, instinctive mind of primitive man. It is the growth of consciousness which we must thank for the existence of problems; they are the Danaän gift of civilization. It is just man's turning away from instinct – his opposing himself to instinct – that creates consciousness. Instinct is nature and seeks to perpetuate nature, whereas consciousness can only seek culture or its denial . . .

Everything in us that still belongs to nature shrinks away from a problem, for its name is doubt, and wherever doubt holds sway there is uncertainty and the possibility of divergent ways. And where several ways seem possible, there we have turned away from the certain guidance of instinct and are handed over to fear. For consciousness is now called upon to do that which nature has always done for her children – namely, to give a certain, unquestionable, and unequivocal decision. And here we are beset by an all-too-human fear that consciousness – our Promethean conquest – may in the end not be able to serve us as well as nature.

Problems thus draw us into an orphaned and isolated state where we are abandoned by nature and are driven to consciousness. There is no other way open to us; we are forced to resort to conscious decisions and solutions where formerly we trusted ourselves to natural happenings. Every problem, therefore, brings the possibility of a widening of consciousness, but also the necessity of saying goodbye to childlike unconsciousness and trust in nature. This necessity is a psychic fact of such importance that it constitutes one of the most essential symbolic teachings of the Christian religion. It is the sacrifice of the merely natural man, of the unconscious, ingenuous being whose tragic career began with the eating of the apple in Paradise.

The biblical fall of man presents the dawn of consciousness as a curse. And as a matter of fact it is in this light that we first look upon every problem that forces us to greater consciousness and separates us even further from the paradise of unconscious childhood. Every one of us gladly turns away from his problems; if possible, they must not be mentioned, or, better still, their existence is denied. We wish to make our lives simple, certain, and smooth, and for that reason problems are taboo. ('The Stages of Life', *CW* 8: 750–1)

For Jung, problems are characteristic of consciousness, and consciousness develops mainly when there are problems to solve. Problems produce tension in the psyche and this generates creativity. However, in the 'instinctive mind of primitive man', which Jung associates with an unconscious condition, there are relatively few problems. In the instinctive state, nature thinks for us and we remain faithful to it. Instinct rules supreme and we are drawn along in its path, like mechanisms responding to the laws of necessity.

Instinct has the advantage of being automatic and not requiring conscious effort. But under instinct we are not free to act, decide or choose. There is no capacity to widen our consciousness, nor is it possible to separate from the collective. Instinct makes us conventional and conformist, because we are doing what has already been decided for us.

For Jung, the development of consciousness throughout our lives is based on a conflictual model. Consciousness arises as we become aware of opposite forces at work in the self. The role of consciousness is to adjudicate on conflicts and decide how they are to be resolved. The tension generated from the conflict is what drives consciousness forward. When we develop our capacity for reflection, conflicts that were previously latent become manifest. The rise of consciousness puts an end to the smooth, uninterrupted flow of natural life. This is a problematical gift, yet it provides the energy needed for the development of personality and civilization.

To the extent that we remain unconscious we support the forces of inertia. Why would we subvert our humanity and ruin our development? Jung suggests that we fear consciousness may not be able to guide us through, and that the merely human light of consciousness will be snuffed out by the problems we encounter. We fear our civilization might not prove as reliable a guide as nature. In dark moments shrouded with uncertainty, the child within us cries out for the surer path of nature and the certainty of instinct. Yet rage as we might against our isolation, we have no alternative but to tread the path we are on. There is no going back, Jung asserts, only a movement forward.

The myths of the West reveal an original state of innocence (Eden), a painful fall into experience (Exile), and a need to move beyond to a new, third state (Redemption). These stages are central to the creation mythology of Judaism, Christianity and Islam. Jung reads this mythology as a psychological process. First we have innocent unconsciousness, a condition which is idealized in most traditions. Then we have the state in which we are cast out of Eden, and suffer the many problems that beset us when a heavenly Creator no longer protects us.

For Jung, the fall from Eden is necessary. Although unconsciousness is idealized as paradise, we are not free to experiment with nature or ourselves. The serpent promises that if we eat from the forbidden fruit, our eyes will be opened and we will be like gods, knowing good and evil. That is, we will acquire the gift of consciousness and be free to know more about the world, but this will come at the cost of our unity with nature. Jung sees our disobedience to God as necessary. The 'will of God' would be synonymous with nature, an immutable law. Any departure from this law is experienced by the nascent consciousness as a transgression of order.

In Jung's view, the creation story reflects our awareness of our insufficiency. Something has been unleashed in the act of consciousness which fills us with fear. It is as if we have sinned against God, moved contrary to the way things ought to be. Consciousness is experienced initially as a vice, as a transgression against the good, mainly because it makes us feel so bad. We feel conflicted, divided, fragmented. We are expelled from the Garden and uncertain of our way forward.

But, difficult as it is, we cannot go back. Our future course is to a new kind of freedom. For Jews, this freedom is the possibility of transcending exile through atonement. For Christians, this freedom is in entering a new relationship with God through the person of Christ, who is the Second Adam, a figure who restores unity with God through his passion. For Muslims, a new relationship with Allah is achieved through the life and struggle of Mohammed and the prophetic tradition. Each Abrahamic tradition presents the fall from a state of grace, and explores the possibility of healing the relationship with the creator in a new way. No Western tradition advocates a reversal of the historical process, a denial of our suffering through creeping back to the Garden.

True to his Abrahamic background, Jung postulated a transcendental element that facilitates our journey towards wholeness. This element, or archetype, Jung calls the *Self*, and it acts as an invisible guarantor of the ego as it makes its journey through life. The word 'Self' is perhaps an odd choice of term for something that is essentially *other* than the ego. For Jung, the ego is the centre of consciousness, the focus of our personal identity, whereas the Self is the centre of the entire psyche, conscious and unconscious, and thus the focus of our transpersonal identity. The ego stands to the Self in Jung's system as humanity to God.

In Jungian literature, the Self is capitalized to distinguish it from the everyday usage of 'self', as in 'myself', 'himself' and so on. It is therefore a highly technical and specific term in Jung's psychology. It has no equivalent in the Freudian system, and its closest counterpart is the *Atman* or 'God within', of Hindu philosophy. The Self is not the same as Jung's No. 2 personality, because the former includes the ego as one of its organs, whereas the latter is an expression only of the unconscious mind.

The Self is virtually a transcendental concept, and it cannot be known directly by the ego, but only indirectly through symbol, dream and myth. In the idea of the Self, it is as if Jung is reinventing the concept of a redeemer for a psychological age. He wants us to think of Christ, atonement and redemption as precursors of a new experience that we are just beginning to glimpse in scientific terms. The archetype of the Self stands behind all of Jung's work, and represents the origin of the ego and the goal to which every ego strives. From the standpoint of the Self, the ego is a working hypothesis. The ego has no substantive reality, but is an enabling fiction that allows something greater to express itself.

Jung believed that in the first half of life the ego needs to stabilize and adjust itself to family, world and society. Then, according to his theory, the ego is displaced at about the middle of life, to allow for the greater element to emerge. This idea has become widely popularized as the so-called *midlife crisis*. Jung employs the metaphor of the rise and descent of the sun to describe our life's course:

> In order to characterize [this change within the psyche] I must take for comparison the daily course of the sun . . . In the morning it rises from the nocturnal sea of unconsciousness and looks upon the wide, bright world which lies before it in an expanse that steadily widens the higher it climbs in the firmament. In this extension of its field of action caused by its own rising, the sun will discover its significance; it will see the attainment of the greatest possible height . . . as its goal. At the stroke of noon the descent begins. And the descent means the reversal of all the ideals and values that were cherished in the morning. The sun falls into contradiction with itself. It is as though

it should draw in its rays instead of emitting them. (*CW* 8: 778)

Jung admits that all comparisons fall short, but the course of the sun occurred to him as a likely metaphor for the rise and fall of the human ego. The ego must rise and fall, else the Self does not appear, or is inhibited in its appearance. Individuation is thus similar to the 'way of the Cross' in Christianity, or the path of suffering in mysticism.

The paradoxical feature of this theory is that the ego needs the Self for its fulfilment, but the Self needs the ego for its expression and incarnation in the world. Without the ego, the Self has no purchase on life, no entry into time and space. Hence, the Self does not wish to crush the ego; the ego is the Self's messenger or servant. The ego has to feel stable and adjusted to reality, even if this stability is illusory and soon to be swept away. The purpose of the first half of life is to give the ego a sense of security, and to make it believe in its achievements. The ego is the agent of incarnation, and if it does not feel grounded the Self cannot begin its work.

Jung's theory is slightly dated and reflects a time in which society was more stable than it is today. The ego nowadays is not given the luxury of developing itself for thirty-five years, unimpeded by disruptions. A contemporary Jungian psychology will need to take into account that these two processes, solidifying the ego and displacing the ego, may need to be thought of as parallel developments, or as simultaneous movements in which now one and now the other predominates. The theory of the stages of life needs some postmodern modifications, in my view.

With the collapse of so many traditions and forms of social containment, the modern ego is unable to feel secure in society for up to half a lifetime. We often find that even very young people have to go in search of meaning and purpose, since these elements are no longer evident in or provided by society, and have to be sought by individual effort. Ironically, secular society, by alienating us from religious truth, is unwittingly turning more and more people into mystics and visionaries, because the need for spiritual meaning is innate, and when society no longer provides it, we have to help ourselves. [24]

Although Jung's theory asserts that a displacement of ego needs to take place at midlife, this is by no means always the case. The mature ego is full of its own status and defences and does whatever it can to avoid displacement. The ego takes the illusion of its power and stability quite seriously, and strives to protect itself against likely attack from the forces of the Self. The ego forgets that its role is secondary or instrumental, and it thinks that life is meant to serve it. Under secular conditions, the belief that the ego is 'number one' is reinforced by social attitudes, media influence, capitalism and consumerism.

> The nearer we approach to the middle of life, and the better we have succeeded in entrenching ourselves in our personal attitudes and social positions, the more it appears as if we had discovered the right course and the right ideals and principles of behaviour. For this reason we suppose them to be eternally valid, and make a virtue of unchangeably clinging to them. (CW 8: 772)

By the time the ego reaches midlife, there are hardly any signs in the secular landscape that remind it of its true role. What greater reality? What higher authority? The ego sees little of this, because it has forgotten the past and does not know how to read the present. The cost of living in a nonreligious world is that we construct a world based on ego values and forget to ask 'What is it for?'

> The very aim of religious education, from the exhortation to put off the old Adam right back to the rebirth rituals of primitive races, is to transform the human being into the new, future man, and to allow the old to die away. (*CW* 8: 766)

The absence of sacred stories makes it all the more difficult for transformation to occur and less likely that it will do so, at least voluntarily.

Life is full of suffering but with a comic theme underneath. Just as we have begun to figure out how reality works, and how to succeed at the game of life, we are made aware of a new set of rules, a different game. We are not just playing a game of the ego, with its goal of social adjustment, but a game of the soul, with its goal of adjustment to spirit. This can create dismay and disorientation in many lives.

In Jung's view, the midlife crisis visits all of us, but some of us manage to ward it off, with as many resources as we can find. A typical response at midlife is to rigidify the ego and reject the Self. The ego goes into a state of alarm and erects barriers. Dreams can dramatize this situation: a civil war breaks out between rival groups, and each side accuses the other of atrocities and evils. Or people are outside the house, wanting to come in, but we erect shutters and boards to keep them out, and install security devices to keep out the unwanted parties. The ego does not give up its power without a fight.

We resist the Self because we have become familiar with ourselves as one person and not two. However, the Self has an energy-value equal to the ego, and once activated it 'can on occasion wrest leadership' from the ego (*CW* 8: 757). In other words, the Self can find itself with a greater energy potential than the ego, and continued resistance on the part of the ego can lead to catastrophe. Hence the Self must be accommodated, if well-being is to be restored. Resistance must be 'shattered', says Jung, so that we can 'build up a state of wider and higher consciousness' (*CW* 8: 767).

5

THE DARK SIDE IN INDIVIDUALS AND NATIONS

It seems to me that we should take the problem of the unconscious very seriously indeed. The tremendous compulsion towards goodness and the immense moral force of Christianity are not merely an argument in the latter's favour, they are also a proof of the strength of its suppressed and repressed counterpart – the antichristian, barbarian element. The existence within us of something that can turn against us, that can become a serious matter for us, I regard not merely as a dangerous peculiarity, but as a valuable and congenial asset as well. It is a still untouched fortune, an uncorrupted treasure, a sign of youthfulness, an earnest of rebirth. Nevertheless, to value the unconscious exclusively for the sake of its positive qualities and to regard it as a source of revelation would be fundamentally wrong. The unconscious is, first and foremost, the world of the past, which is activated by the one-sidedness of the conscious attitude. Whenever life proceeds one-sidedly in any given direction, the self-regulation of the organism produces in the unconscious an accumulation of all those factors which play too small a part in the individual's conscious existence. For this reason I have put forward the compensation theory of the unconscious as a complement to the repression theory.

The compensatory function . . . is the natural, automatic function of the unconscious and is constantly present. It owes its existence to the simple fact that all the impulses, thoughts, wishes, and tendencies which run counter to the rational orientation of daily life are denied expression, thrust into the background, and finally fall into the unconscious. There all the things which we have repressed and suppressed, which we have deliberately ignored and devalued, gradually accumulate and, in time, acquire such force that they begin to influence consciousness. This influence would be in direct opposition to our conscious orientation if the unconscious consisted only of repressed and suppressed material. But this is not the case. The unconscious also contains the dark springs of instinct and intuition, it contains all those forces which mere reasonableness, propriety, and the orderly course of bourgeois existence could never call awake, all those creative forces which lead man onwards to new developments, new forms, and new goals. The influence of the unconscious . . . adds to consciousness everything that has been excluded by the drying up of the springs of intuition and by the fixed pursuit of a single goal.

This function, as I say, works automatically, but, owing to the notorious atrophy of instinct in civilized man, it is often too weak to swing his one-sided orientation of consciousness in a new direction against the pressures of society . . . When, therefore, unconscious contents accumulate as a result of being consistently ignored, they are

bound to exert an influence that is pathological. ('The Role
of the Unconscious', *CW* 10: 20–26)

Jung's life and work are preoccupied with the 'dark side' of
humanity. It is not that Jung felt that we should celebrate
darkness in a satanic way or become devil worshippers. But he
felt we should enter into the darkness and find out what is
inside it. Like Freud and Nietzsche, Jung felt Western civilization had been celebrating and emphasizing the 'light' for
too long. Christianity purports to be a religion of the light,
and has encouraged us to turn away from darkness. According
to Jung, this has had a negative effect on the psyche and body,
and disturbed the flow of energy in the body–psyche. When
civilization decides that the dark is bad, and to be suppressed,
the natural gradient of life is upset.

The term 'dark side' has reached popular awareness
through the *Star Wars* series, and the films borrowed the term
from Jung, through the discussions between director George
Lucas and Jungian scholar Joseph Campbell. Jung sometimes
referred to the dark side as the *shadow*, and he believed that
not only individuals but also whole nations, communities and
groups had 'shadows' that had to be encountered. The more
an individual or group strives for light, the longer and darker
is the shadow that is cast. Jung felt that the shadow has typically been demonized and made evil, rather than viewed in a
philosophical and more fair or equitable light.

It contains, as he says in the passage above, not just the
undesirable elements of life but also the 'dark springs of
instinct and intuition' which 'mere reasonableness' could
never call awake. The shadow is a 'dangerous peculiarity' and
a 'valuable and congenial asset as well'. Some Jungians have
written about the 'gold' in the shadow, believing that what

consciousness rejects is often the stuff of life that gives it its highest value.[25] A civilization that emphasizes the light ends up as pallid, empty, bloodless, superficial, routine, devoid of adventure – but also, as we will see, unprepared for onslaughts of pure evil.

There are several key points to bear in mind in Jung's philosophy of ethics. Good and evil are not fixed or absolute, but are relative and conditioned by society. What consciousness values is called 'good', what it dislikes is 'evil'. However, consciousness cannot always be trusted with such absolute authority. The unconscious introduces a new dimension and may have a very different moral view. This unsettles society, religion and the architects of official morality.

Good and evil can be reversed in psychological experience. For instance, leading a righteous and sinless life, devoid of instinct or libido, may be judged 'good' by religion, but therapy sees it as 'bad', repressive, anti-life and creating the moral conditions for violent explosions of irrationality or sexual abuse. The demise of religious ethics and the rise of a therapeutic ethic is partly to do with society shifting its identification from the 'perfection' ideal of religion to the 'wholeness' ideal of therapy.[26]

An obsessive focus on the good can distort the idea of good and rigidify our worldview. The best therapy we can give ourselves is often to allow an expression of 'evil'. We need to 'give the devil his due'. That which is called 'evil' often dissipates once it is given an outlet. This is because evil is often a distorted version of psychic energy that can be utilized in other ways. For instance, seething hatred for another may be a sign that we have to differentiate ourselves from the other, and find our own identity. Hatred acts as the force that separates what must be separated. If we direct our energy to the positive end of differentiation, we may no longer need to hate the other.

The opening extract was written in 1918, at the end of the Great War. Jung set himself the task of understanding war from a psychological point of view. He was not interested in taking sides, in deeming one side right or wrong, but in asking the psychological question: Where had this eruption of evil come from? What can a psychology of the unconscious contribute to such a catastrophe? Many sociologists, political scientists and theorists would argue that a psychology of the unconscious has little or nothing to offer to the cure of wars. They would argue that social catastrophe could be better understood in terms of known factors, such as wealth, class, economics, political relations and social inequality. Jung understood this point of view, but moved ahead with his interpretation anyway.

His diagnosis is that civilization is out of balance with itself and with nature. It has moved ahead on a course that could be self-destructive. Civilization has privileged rationality above the nonrational, reason above unreason – which sounds logical, but Jung insists is unwise. We suppress too much that does not make sense, and repress too much that seems 'unchristian' or 'immoral', and create a turbulent and violent 'shadow' which is a kind of time-bomb that can explode at any moment. All that is needed is some kind of trigger: economic distress, unwelcome developments abroad or another people whom we dislike. Then we find some kind of political justification for unleashing the internal bomb that has been gathering force for a long time.

The evil within ourselves is experienced first of all through *projection*. Since the idea of possessing evil qualities is abhorrent, we 'project' these qualities upon those around us who are 'more or less suitable objects' (*CW* 10: 41). Jung defines projection as a process whereby 'an unconscious content of the subject . . . is transferred to the object, and there magnifies one of its peculiarities to such proportions that it seems a sufficient cause of the disturbance' (*CW* 10: 41). The enemy is seen as an 'axis' or locus of evil, and this serves to spur on the nation to defeat the opponent. Projection leads to war, violence and devastation, but Jung argued that anything is seen as preferable to recognizing that the sources of evil are within our own nature. We will sacrifice men and women in war, expend material resources and risk lives and the security of the world, but nothing will cause us to make the necessary sacrifice, that is, to adjust our worldview to recognize the existence of evil within our selves, our culture and nation.

Our civilization is courting disaster. By refusing to accept that the human psyche is complex and paradoxical, we have no way of reconciling the opposing forces that gather momentum in our psychic interior. By clinging to ideals of goodness, by assuming we can remain innocent, we have no way of integrating the dark and the ambivalent:

> The tremendous forces unleashed by the war bring about their own destruction because there is no human hand to preserve and guide them. Our view of the world has proved too narrow to channel these forces into a cultural form. (*CW* 10: 31)

We need cultural support to help us understand the forces that arise in ourselves. We need a theory of energy, of polarity and paradox, which is greater than the logical system that currently rules our thinking. Our religion and philosophy are

inadequate to contain the forces that assail us and lead to cata-
clysm and destruction.

What is needed is a more fluid and adaptable moral vision,
a religion that can encompass the dark as well as the light, a
philosophy that helps us come to terms with the paradoxical
forces of the self and creation. Such systems existed in the past,
in Taoism and Confucianism in China, in alchemy and gnosticism in the Middle Eastern world, and Jung believed we
must search for a cosmological system that can encompass the
opposites. The secret is to discover a framework that invites
and not suppresses the inferior elements, that transforms the
forces of the nonrational. Otherwise, we will be destroyed by
what we fail to comprehend. 'We have no imagination for
evil, but evil has us in its grip' (*MDR*: 363). Jung sees the West
as lacking a natural instinct in these matters, a sign of its alienation from nature.

In relation to Germany in 1918, Jung saw a nation that did
not possess a religion capable of containing the pagan forces
that belong to its cultural heritage:

> Christianity split the Germanic barbarian into an upper
> and a lower half, and enabled him, by repressing the
> dark side, to domesticate the brighter half and fit it for
> civilization. But the lower, darker half still awaits
> redemption and a second spell of domestication. Until
> then, it will remain associated with the vestiges of the
> prehistoric age, with the collective unconscious, which is
> subject to a peculiar and ever-increasing activation. As
> the Christian view of the world loses its authority, the
> more menacingly will the 'blond beast' be heard prowling
> about in its underground prison, ready at any moment to
> burst out with devastating consequences. When this happens

> in the individual it brings about a psychological revolu-
> tion, but it can also take a social form. (*CW* 10: 17)

Commentators have referred to the prescience of Jung's statements of 1918, and how they appear to anticipate the spectre of National Socialism and the Nazi uprising (the 'blond beast') in Germany in the 1930s. Just as astonishing, perhaps, is how Jung's analysis seems to predict in detail the revelation given voice in W. B. Yeats's poem, 'The Second Coming' (1920).[27] In this poem, which some critics consider to be the most important of the twentieth century, Yeats shows that the forces of 'evil' are demanding to be accepted into a broader moral worldview, and the 'beast' wants to be 'born' in Bethlehem, and recognized as a cosmic power that is co-equal with the good.

What Jung said about Germany was true for all nations, but Germany expressed the problem of nations in a marked form. Jung said that Christianity works only for one half of the German psyche, the 'brighter half' which is amenable to moral persuasion, education and ethical values. Christianity took the brighter side, domesticated it and made it 'fit for civilization'. But Christianity did not act as a civilizing force upon the whole psyche. It did not engage our darker forces, but 'repressed the dark side' in order to emphasize the light and good.

In Greek terms, we might differentiate between the gods Apollo and Dionysus. Christianity took hold of our Apollonic side, our capacity for order and reason, and gave this direction, but our Dionysian side, our capacity for disorder and ecstatic activity, was neglected. Christianity hoped that the Dionysian forces would fall into line behind the Apollonic, that desire would follow reason, that instinct and passion would be guided to a higher destiny.

Jung is grateful for the contribution of Christianity, but sees it as largely ineffectual. For him, it is a kind of wishful thinking. 'If only' people would be good; 'if only' we would turn the other cheek; 'if only' we could live as if we had desires for order, culture, harmony and not Dionysian desires for disorder, instinct, unreason, passion, selfishness and so on. Jung argued that our civilization extends only so far into the psyche, and beneath the 'pleasing patina' we are as primitive as ever: 'the lower, darker half still awaits redemption and a second spell of domestication'.

The 'beast' or antichrist in humanity is demanding new expression, and will no longer be content with Christian repression. In Yeats's famous poem, the beast is already on its new journey into consciousness, and wanting to be recognized as sacred: it is 'slouching towards Bethlehem to be born'. In the modern arts and in philosophy, there is the constant theme that our time requires a fundamental rebirth of the dark side as a cosmic principle and not merely as a nuisance to be expunged. We have to view darkness with greater respect, and learn to appreciate not only its capacity for destruction, but its capacity for vitality, growth and transformation.

If we don't do anything about this, we will be destroyed by outbursts of irrationality and unreason, such as we see in war, terrorism and violence. Hence the most important act for the future is to become aware of our darkness, to lower our moral sights, to resist the desire to be perfect, to recognize our complexity, to become critical of conventional morality, and to search for a new balance that includes our dark side as well as the light. Such psychological development, Jung believed, starts with individuals who have the courage to accept their personal darkness, and then it moves out from them to the larger social sphere. He was pessimistic about such change originating from above, by government decree or religious ideologies, and felt that true change always begins from below.

6

GENDER AND ARCHETYPE

The projection-making factor is the anima, or rather the unconscious as represented by the anima. Whenever she appears, in dreams, visions, and fantasies, she takes on personified form, thus demonstrating that the factor she embodies possesses all the outstanding characteristics of a feminine being. She is not an invention of the conscious, but a spontaneous product of the unconscious. Nor is she a substitute figure for the mother. On the contrary, there is every likelihood that the numinous qualities which make the mother-imago so dangerously powerful derive from the collective archetype of the anima, which is incarnated anew in every male child.

Since the anima is an archetype that is found in men, it is reasonable to suppose that an equivalent archetype must be present in women; for just as the man is compensated by a feminine element, so the woman is compensated by a masculine one. I do not, however, wish this argument to give the impression that these compensatory relationships were arrived at by deduction. On the contrary, long and varied experience was needed in order to grasp the nature of anima and animus empirically. Whatever we have to say about these archetypes, therefore, is either directly verifiable or at least rendered probable by the facts. At the same time, I am fully aware that we are discussing pioneer work which by its very nature can only be provisional.

Just as the mother seems to be the first carrier of the projection-making factor for the son, so is the father for the daughter. Practical experience of these relationships is made up of many individual cases presenting all kinds of variations on the same basic theme. A concise description of them can, therefore, be no more than schematic.

Woman is compensated by a masculine element and therefore her unconscious has, so to speak, a masculine imprint. This results in a considerable psychological difference between men and women, and accordingly I have called the projection-making factor in women the animus, which means mind or spirit. The animus corresponds to the paternal Logos just as the anima corresponds to the maternal Eros. But I do not wish or intend to give these two intuitive concepts too specific a definition. I use Eros and Logos merely as conceptual aids to describe the fact that woman's consciousness is characterized more by the connective quality of Eros than by the discrimination and cognition associated with Logos. In men, Eros, the function of relationship, is usually less developed than Logos. In women, on the other hand, Eros is an expression of their true nature, while their Logos is often only a regrettable accident. ('The Syzygy: Anima and Animus', *CW* 9, Part 2: 26–29)

Jung's views on gender move in a different direction to most contemporary thinking. The idea that gender is constructed by society enjoys wide currency today, but Jung believed that gender was largely a result of psychological and biological influences. For him, gender differences have more to do with universal archetypes than with social stereotypes, although both archetypes and stereotypes could be seen to play important determining roles in gender. That is, nurture (society) and nature (psychobiology) are both major players in this work of construction. In the big picture, in which universals are granted a place alongside social particulars, Jung's contribution is valuable and has a great deal to offer.

For Jung, masculinity and femininity are *principles* of the human psyche, and by 'principles' he meant essential elements or constitutive qualities of the mind. Masculinity and femininity are for him coexisting and complementary (if at times conflicting) cosmic forces, similar to the interplay of yin and yang in Taoist philosophy. Masculine and feminine principles express themselves mythologically as gods and goddesses, and Jung believed we would do well to recover spiritual respect for these forces lost in Christianity. We have, he believed, 'humanized' these cosmic principles by losing sight of the sacred forms that once contained them, and in modern times we have not sufficiently recognized that we are dealing with forces that are greater than ourselves.

He argued that women are governed by a feminine principle which he called *eros*, a Greek term for connectedness and love, and men are ruled by a masculine principle, *logos*, which in this context he associated with discrimination and cognition. For Jung, the male must realize and actualize his masculine logos, and not merely assume it is given by his genes or biology. Males have to *become* men, and females *become* women, so that the claiming of one's gendered identity is at the same time a personal quest and psychological adventure.

This connects Jung's thought with the initiation ceremonies of all traditional and indigenous peoples. Such cultures have long understood that the attainment of masculinity for boys and femininity for girls is a personal achievement, to be facilitated by cultural rites of passage and religious ceremonies. The beginning of adolescence is seen as the right moment to induct girls and boys into the adult religious mysteries that are connected with their spiritual identity and with their sexual development at this crucial moment in their lives. In these rituals, masculinity is mythologized as a god or paternal spirit, and femininity as a goddess or maternal spirit. To become a man is to enter the archetypal field of the god or spiritual father, and to become a woman is to come into contact with sacred feminine forces.

Jung supported the recovery of this kind of ritual in the modern world, and he believed that masculinity and femininity had been desacralized and taken for granted in our society. Jung's views on gender have led to the establishment of 'archetypal' (sometimes called 'spiritual') men's and women's movements, especially in the United States, where the response to Jung's writings on gender seems to be most strongly felt. These movements, led by such figures as Robert Bly, James Hillman, Robert Moore, Marion Woodman and Jean Shinoda Bolen, seek to recover the archetypal basis of gender, and to resacralize the experience of being men and women.[28] They advocate getting in touch with ancient gods or goddesses, with the 'wild' man or woman in the unconscious, and they frequently hold 'workshops' in desert or wilderness places, so that people can experiment with ritual and ceremony, often borrowing from the initiatory practices of tribal cultures. Such women's and men's movements are sometimes parodied on television shows because there is a general fear about their impact in modern society. However, like them or not, they represent parallel or alternative movements to the better-known gender movements related to mainstream political and social liberations.

Jung was especially concerned that boys and men were unable to realize their masculinity in a time that offered few rites of passage. He was concerned because young males are emotionally attached to their mothers as the primary caregivers, and seem to require social or ceremonial support to claim their masculine identity from the embrace of the mother. Girls share the same gender as their mothers, and the need for separation is not as great. Jung believed this is why women's rituals of initiation are typically not as violent or dramatic as those of men, where *proving* masculinity has been a major issue for so long (CW 5: 419). If boys do not manage to separate from their mothers, the result is effeminacy, stunted or retarded emotional development, and impaired conscious focus, all of which tally with Freud's views on what he called the unresolved Oedipal complex.

Jung's anxiety about masculinity seems ironic in a time so influenced by feminism's vision of a society controlled by male dominance and strength. However, Jung would argue that the masculine mystique of Western society is a social persona which must not be confused with the attainment of a mature masculinity. As feminism and social progress work to undermine the patriarchal order, men and boys are still left with the primary psychological task of securing their masculinity and wresting their identity from the mother-complex. Jung argued that men do not need shows of bravado or machismo when they feel secure in their masculinity and have broken free from the mother. Although his theories appear to contradict the feminist position initially, Jung seeks a social and psychological world in which gender equality and balance can be discovered.

For Jung, archetype and gender operate at two levels: in the claiming of our conscious identity as men and women (logos and eros), and in the exploration of our unconscious identity (anima and animus), where we meet the opposite forces to those that rule in the conscious realm. Jung was a pioneer in the study of psychosexuality, and his argument that men had a feminine side or anima, and women a masculine side or animus, was advanced and socially challenging for the 1920s. Having discovered the contrasexual element in the psychology of men and women, Jung was concerned to limit and contain this potentially disruptive element. A conventional gender identity had to be preserved, even though elements of the opposite sexual polarity were to be allowed.

If men showed too much femininity, especially in the choice of a homosexual partner, Jung would express disapproval and suspect such men of suffering from a mother-complex, of stifling their masculine development and of being 'anima possessed'. If women became too masculine, Jung would refer to them as 'opinionated', 'irritating' and 'animus ridden'. Jung would say that men and women who showed these traits were 'acting out' the contrasexual element, and had not yet achieved healthy integration.

Jung made it clear that men must not identify with the anima (eros) or view it as their essential nature; nor must women identify with the animus (logos) and assume that it is their true identity. His view was that the contrasexual nature had to be integrated into a personality that remained basically masculine (for men) and feminine (for women).

The notion of a quiet, discreet, nondisruptive integration of the contrasexual element in men and women is an abstract proposition which does not have the atmosphere of reality about it. Jung's theories provide an explicit foundation for what many have called the feminization of men and the masculinization of women, but he would like us to be fully integrated rather than displaying our lack of integration in public.

> Just as the anima becomes, through integration, the Eros of consciousness, so the animus becomes a Logos; and in the same way that the anima gives relationship and relatedness to a man's consciousness, the animus gives to woman's consciousness a capacity for reflection, deliberation, and self-knowledge. (*CW* 9, 2: 33)

How this revolution of personality and identity will occur without major disruption to gender norms and moral standards is not discussed. It is clear that Jung regarded as unseemly any experimentation with established patterns of behaviour, even though his own theories made it inevitable that increased fluidity and plurality in gender norms would arise as soon as a general activation of the unconscious had taken place in patriarchal society. Jung's views seemed simultaneously radical, in their bold advocacy of a bisexual potential in the human personality, and conservative, in their insistence that psychological integration should occur without much disturbance to the social or political sphere. In his cautionary essay, 'Women in Europe' (1927), he wrote: 'A man should live as a man and a woman as a woman' (*CW* 10: 243).

Much anger and resentment has built up over time to Jung's archetypal theory in its application to gender. I agree with Jung's critics that some of what he took to be archetypal, and *given* by life, was in fact stereotypical and conditioned by society. The very notion that men are governed by a single principle, logos, and women, eros, is unwanted news in our pluralistic and experimental age. Jung's argument that contrasexual forces in the unconscious compensate men and women is cold comfort to a society which does not want men or women to be stereotyped in the first place. Men are by no means confined in their conscious styles to thinking or logos, and women are no longer bound by society to express feeling, social concern or connectedness.

The bonds of traditional conditioning have weakened considerably since Jung's death in 1961, and since then we have seen a series of social revolutions that have radicalized and diversified social behaviour. What looked like fixed or biological reality is now viewed as social conditioning. Men are free today to enter the realm of Eros, who, after all, is a male god in Greek mythology. The behavioural styles of women have diversified since Jung's time, and the notion that women can only engage in thinking through an unconscious (and inferior) animus is no longer plausible. However, I disagree with those people who want to throw out Jung's vision entirely. His model of the psyche as a field of psychosexual forces that move in and out of balance, and tend towards self-regulation and compensation, is a powerful one that we cannot afford to lose. We can keep his vision of archetypal energies without holding the rigid formula that they first came in. To lose altogether the archetypal dimension of gender is too great a loss.

In the early 1970s James Hillman shed new light on the problem by arguing that Jung had contradicted his theory. One cannot claim that archetypes are universal and assert that they are found in one gender but not in another. Archetypes are either original predispositions in the human psyche, or they are not. In *The Myth of Analysis* Hillman said it was not possible to assume that all men are governed by logos, all women by eros. Similarly, it was spurious to argue that only men have animas or souls, and only women animuses or spirits. He wrote:

> The *archetype* of the anima cannot be limited to the special psychology of men, since the archetypes transcend both men and women and their biological differences and social roles.[29]

Archetypes are larger than gender and cannot be confined to it. Postmodern readers of Jung use Jung's own logic to explode his early formula, in which 'archetypes' looked suspiciously like stereotypes. A great deal of creativity in Jungian studies has centred on the deconstruction of Jung's formula, while maintaining his insights about psychosexuality and the role of the unconscious in mirroring the opposite polarity to consciousness. This more recent work, often described as post-Jungian, can be found in the writings of Andrew Samuels, Susan Rowland, Demaris Wehr, Sue Austin and others.[30] Jung's insights need to be resituated in a psychology that includes the social discoveries of the last fifty years, with greater awareness of individual difference, gender fluidity and moral relativity.

Some of the negative reaction to Jung on gender is due to the language he used. When Jung says the anima is 'inferior' in men, that she is a 'degenerate woman', he is speaking in a forthright manner about things that we would express differently today. Similarly, when Jung argued that the animus in women is inferior, he is not wishing to suggest that the animus is inherently inferior, or that women are cursed with constitutional inferiority. He is speaking a technical language about the relative insufficiency of these archetypes while they remain in an unconscious and undeveloped condition.

Readers today often find Jung's remarks to be blunt or insulting, as for instance: 'In women, Eros is an expression of their true nature, while their Logos is often only a regrettable accident.' Later he writes: 'No matter how friendly and obliging a woman's Eros may be, no logic on earth can shake her if she is ridden by the animus.' The offence caused by such language is enough to turn many readers away, but if we can understand his core concepts, and not focus entirely on their insensitive expression, we should be able to maintain a psychodynamic model of gender that is useful in practical terms.

Jung was a fierce individualist whose passion was to achieve recognition for the reality of the psyche, and for the continued existence of sacred forces in a desacralized world. His aim was the integration of psychosexual forces within a dynamic wholeness, envisaged psychologically as the realization of the Self. For Jung, the problem of accepting the contrasexual element of the unconscious was less a political issue related to the stability of society or the challenging of social norms, than it was a practical or therapeutic issue about how the patient can maintain his or her integrity while coming to terms with that which is essentially other than the ego. It was as if, for Jung, the Self was insisting on a new development that the human ego was not yet capable of understanding.

The ego, he believed, was constantly in danger of being disoriented by the realization that it was essentially 'two persons', and not one. He could see patients becoming insecure and anxious about what the unconscious was saying to them. A man would be filled with fear and near panic at the thought that he was 'also' a woman, or had an internal personality that corresponded to the 'minority of female genes in his biological make-up' (*CW* 18: 429). Jung attempted to downplay the social revolutionary implications of his theories, partly to avoid panic breaking out in his patients and readers. He was telling them that they were plural, and yet they wanted to be told that they were already whole.

Jung's conviction was that to achieve wholeness, one first has to go through the experience of fragmentation and experience the many parts of which the psyche is composed. The normal ego prefers stability and single-mindedness to the challenge of plurality and fragmentation, and that is why Jung argued that the sooner we can overcome the normal ego, and aspire to the realization of the Self, the more whole we might become and the less terrified we would be of the fragmented parts that rise to meet us from the unconscious.

Sometimes, he argued, the Self is symbolized in dreams and artwork as androgynous, because it points to a wholeness that transcends the ego and its gender. Theologically, he felt the divine should be imagined as both masculine and feminine, so that human beings could focus upon a higher symbol that combines the opposites.

7

NEUROSIS, THERAPY AND INDIVIDUATION

The remarkable potency of unconscious contents always indicates a corresponding weakness in the conscious mind and its functions. It is as though the latter were threatened with impotence. For primitive man this danger is one of the most terrifying instances of 'magic'. So we can understand why this secret fear is also to be found among civilized people. In serious cases it is the secret fear of going mad; in less serious, the fear of the unconscious – a fear which even the normal person exhibits in his resistance to psychological views and explanations.

The doctor knows these well-defended zones from his consulting hours: they are reminiscent of island fortresses from which the neurotic tries to ward off the octopus. ('Happy neurosis island,' as one of my patients called his conscious state!) The doctor is well aware that the patient needs an island and would be lost without it. It serves as a refuge for his consciousness and as the last stronghold against the threatening embrace of the unconscious. The same is true of the normal person's taboo regions which psychology must not touch. But since no war was ever won

> on the defensive, one must, in order to terminate hostilities, open negotiations with the enemy and see what his terms really are.
>
>   Such is the intention of the doctor who volunteers to act as a mediator. He is far from wishing to disturb the somewhat precarious island idyll or pull down the fortifications. On the contrary, he is thankful that somewhere a firm foothold exists that does not first have to be fished up out of the chaos, always a desperately difficult task. He knows that the island is a bit cramped and that life on it is pretty meagre and plagued with all sorts of imaginary wants because too much life has been left outside, and that as a result a terrifying monster is created, or rather roused out of its slumbers. He also knows that this seemingly alarming animal stands in a secret compensatory relationship to the island and could supply everything that the island lacks.
> ('The Psychology of the Transference', *CW* 16: 374)

For Jung, the personality is constantly getting stuck in narrow limits, unable to move forward, and is menaced by an *other*, an antagonist who stands in its path. This other is what psychotherapy calls a neurosis, that is, an emotional disorder in which feelings of anxiety, obsessional thoughts, compulsive acts and physical complaints dominate the personality. The aim of therapy is not exactly to get rid of the neurosis, but to transform and deepen it by understanding why it arose in the first place.

Typically, a neurosis emerges when a person's consciousness is not broad enough to encompass the contents of the psyche that demand to be lived and seek expression. The psyche does not tolerate artificial constriction, caused for instance by a morbidly narrow moral view, by an inadequate self-image or by attitudes that stifle and abuse the energies of the personality. The unlived life manifests in neurotic form, and within the neurosis lie the answers that the patient seeks:

> A neurosis is truly removed only when it has removed the false attitude of the ego. We do not cure it – it cures us. A man is ill, but the illness is nature's attempt to heal him, and what the neurotic flings away as absolutely worthless contains the true gold we should never have found elsewhere. (CW 10: 361)

Jung warns against the patient and doctor conspiring against the neurosis in a bid to restore the patient to so-called normality. As repellent as it appears, we have to learn to embrace the neurosis, which is indeed 'nature's attempt to heal [us]', or as he writes elsewhere: 'There is no illness that is not at the same time an unsuccessful attempt at a cure' (CW 15: 68).

The neurotic symptom is secretly the 'true gold'. Jung indirectly refers to alchemy, to his belief that psychotherapy is a modern version of the traditional science of alchemy. In alchemy, the process begins with an unpromising lump of lead, or a base metal substance, and operations are performed in which the lead is converted into gold. This procedure did not produce real gold; however, Jung argued that common gold was not the object of the process. In his view, the alchemist sought philosophical gold or, rather, the Philosopher's Stone (CW 12). This Stone is for Jung a symbol of the Self, and the alchemist was engaged in psychological procedures that help to illuminate how we today might convert a neurotic disorder into a transformed personality.

A patient seeks therapy because something unpleasant has

arisen in his or her life, and the patient's first thought is how to get rid of the burden and assume a normal life. However, Jung believes that the psyche has another perspective, and a different objective. The psyche rarely shares the ego's point of view, but asks for an altogether different outlook, a higher expectation and a more profound goal. The psyche's objective is not normality or social adjustment, but individuation, namely, encouraging the ego to embark on an adventure, to take part in a quest, and to make an effort to understand the breadth and depth of life.

The therapist's role, according to Jung, is to represent the intentionality of the psyche, which the patient is at present unable to comprehend. The ego which finds itself saddled with a neurosis is itself part of the problem. The ego cannot reason its way out of the dilemma, because the ego's limited reason is what led to the difficulty in the first place. The ego thinks it is protecting itself against the annihilating powers of the psyche by constructing a refuge, an 'island fortress', in which it can be at rest. However, this self-care system of the ego is actually a menace in disguise, and a block to the devel- opmental process.[31] Although a 'safe' place, it is far too narrow, and the effect of this refuge is to force the energies of the psyche to adopt an even more hostile appearance in their attempt to break it down.

Jungian therapy is sensitive to interior process, and tries to find the right moment to make interventions. The appropri- ate time must be found to allow the deconstruction of the ego to take place. If it is not the right moment, the process of unravelling can be fatal, and lead to disintegration and the release of the waters of chaos into the psyche. In this sensitive art, the therapist has to be on two sides at the same time, a dif- ficult act to perform. The therapist has to support the patient in his or her conscious position – if this does not occur, the patient will assume the therapist is a destructive influence, and something to run away from.

However, the therapist also needs to take the side of the unconscious, for he or she sees that the unconscious needs to be supported in its attempt to seek expression in a life that has excluded too much psychic reality. As Jung says in the opening passage, the therapist acts as 'mediator' between competing forces, and the task of therapy is to broker a deal that both parties, conscious and unconscious, can live with.

The unlived life accumulates in the unconscious, and it accepts this condition for some time, until it can take no more. The appearance of a neurosis, Jung writes, is a sign that the psyche is still on the side of life. If a neurosis does not occur, then we know that either life is being lived to the optimum degree or, on the contrary, that the psyche has atrophied and been reduced to such an extent that its compensatory function no longer operates. Psychic energy can become so depleted that neurosis does not occur, and the person has no way of knowing that a fatal accident or devastating situation is just around the corner. In such cases, the failure to generate a neurosis can lead to schizophrenia, a far more serious splitting of the mind in which healing is problematical because the psyche has regressed to an archaic level.

Jung rarely lost hope in the therapeutic situation. Even if a psychosis erupted, he would insist that healing could take place, so long as the understanding of the patient could be sought and enlisted. When individuation takes on this darker tone, the dynamics of the psyche become disturbed, but an act of love towards the disturbed figures can lead to almost miraculous reversals of direction. Simply taking the psyche seriously, and acknowledging its reality, 'pays the unconscious a tribute that more or less guarantees its cooperation' (*CW* 9, 2: 40).

At such moments 'big dreams' occur, which Jung believed are designed to restore balance to the psyche, and show us where we have gone wrong. Helpful animals can appear in dreams, to talk to us and indicate a new direction. However, unless we are able to comprehend the symbolism, we may be no better off than before. The psyche can try as hard as it can to restore balance, but unless the conscious mind is willing to follow the guidance, no healing will take place.

Jung says we should learn to welcome the self-division that arises from the psyche's opposition, because we know that we are being 'saved' from the egotistical life, and introduced to a new way of being. This is a process of intuition that reveals more of who we are, more of what we are becoming:

> In psychological language we would say: the problematical state, the inner division with oneself, arises when, side by side with the series of ego-contents, a second series of equal intensity comes into being. This second series, because of its energy-value, has a functional significance equal to that of the ego-complex; we might call it another, second ego which can on occasion even wrest the leadership from the first. This produces the division with oneself, the state that betokens a problem. (*CW* 8: 757)

This 'second ego' confronts the ego like an intruder, a foreign body, an unfamiliar partner. Our task is to befriend the non-ego, to become familiar with it, to realize that our life is also its life. As Jung writes: 'The individual is faced with the necessity of recognizing and accepting what is different and strange as a part of his own life, as a kind of "also-I"' (*CW* 8: 764).

A general rule of individuation is that psychic life that is not being lived 'coagulates' into various oppositional forms, and confronts us as a hostile opponent. The alchemical art is to 'dissolve' the forms that have coagulated, releasing the energy to the person, and making that energy available for life. Jung found alchemical ideas of great therapeutic assistance in working with the (mal)formations of psychic life and their subsequent transformations into more productive states. Jung advises us to look for the opposite of the ego, and to get to know our enemy. It is a kind of martial art: something comes towards us with destructive force, and our task is to avoid a collision, and use the energy of the opponent for our benefit.

The whole of Jung's theory of individuation can be seen as a management of conflict and opposition. Whether we refer to the shadow, the anima or animus, the father or mother, the trickster, or any other archetype, all greet the ego as formations of psychic energy that at first seem opposed to the ego's directions. Through psychological awareness, the ego realizes that these strangers are parts of its larger personality, and that they must be welcomed to the banquet of life – or accommodated on the island of consciousness. Jung argued that it is imperative that the ego maintains its ground, and does not identify with any one of the figures which arise in the course of individuation. Nor, on the other hand, should the ego rigidly defend its island fortress, which would aggravate the process of wholeness and force the psychic figures into increased hostility.

Between these extremes, of identifying with the inner figures and alienating them, lies the desired response, which is that of creative dialogue. Through dream analysis, active imagination, journal work and reflection, the ego enters into dialogue with the interior figures, thus befriending them and drawing them into a circle of friendship. Only in this way, in which the inner figures are incorporated into an expanded consciousness, are we able to break the deadlock between conscious and unconscious and move into a creative exchange.

Jung argued that a psychic *function* breaks the deadlock between the opposites and allows the new to come into being. He called this the *transcendent function*, and it appears to be triggered by high levels of tension that accumulate in the psyche. Jung believed this function arises from the archetype of the Self, and that the Self breaks down opposition by taking the conflict to a higher level, in which the positions of the ego and its enemy are dissolved into a new unity.

Jung seems to be following the thinking of the German philosopher Hegel. It was Hegel who argued that the only way a battle could cease between a thesis and an antithesis was through the construction of a *synthesis* that would include elements from both sides and transcend the opposition. Although Jung denied that Hegel was an influence on his thought, it is hard to imagine Jungian thought without the Hegelian model that sees conflict overcome through the creation of a transcendent 'third' which is neither thesis nor antithesis but a new entity in which both are included.

The term 'transcendent function' can be misleading. Jung does not wish to imply that this is a metaphysical process or a product of spiritual transcendence. Rather, he sees this as a natural and biological process, in which opposition is transcended through the activation of a third 'supraordinate' factor. For instance, a moral conflict in which one is torn between good and evil may be resolved by establishing a third position which brings the devil and the angel in one's nature into relationship. The good side might read this as a defeat or compromise, but the Self is likely to regard it as a triumph of integration and wholeness.

The ego almost never likes this third position, because it seems to include more psychic reality than the ego would allow. The creation of the third, or *tertium* as Jung called it, is almost a biological form of transcendence, in which blockages are removed so that life can continue. In human terms, a new Self comes into being, which is sufficiently large and morally mature to integrate the warring elements that had plagued and hounded the old ego.

Another important clinical term in this context is the *transference*. In the construction of a transference or emotional attachment between patient and therapist, the therapist serves as a container of positive and life-supporting energies. The fact that the therapist is present, that he or she is concerned with my welfare, and able to support me at difficult moments in my therapy, serves to constellate the positive forces in the psyche, and to mobilize these for the sake of growth. Although I may feel under siege from the unconscious, and at the brink of nervous collapse, the very fact that the therapist has seen what I am dealing with and has not 'exploded' is an indication that I too can glimpse the forces of opposition and survive.

Jung emphasized the clinical setting as a safe place which encourages the development of the whole person. Eventually, the patient may be able to sacrifice his or her previously constructed safe place for the more creative safe place of therapy. The key to this is psychological expansion and building a larger view of self and world, without entering an *inflated* state where the ego appropriates the new largeness to itself. This expansion without inflation can only happen once the therapeutic situation has been established and interiorized as a positive object in the mind of the patient.

If the patient is unable to trust the forces of healing in his or her psyche, these forces may be trusted indirectly via the positive transference to the therapist. Therapy can and does act as an artificial boost to the process of individuation, an alchemical container or vessel in which the forces of the psyche can be reconfigured in ways that do not lead to violent explosions or psychotic upheavals.

8

THE SPIRITUAL DIMENSION OF HEALING

In the course of the nineteenth century medicine had become, in its methods and theory, one of the disciplines of natural science, and it cherished the same basically philosophical assumption of *material causation*. For medicine, the psyche as a mental 'substance' did not exist, and experimental psychology also did its best to constitute itself a psychology without a psyche . . .

Neuroses are to be influenced or cured by approaching them not from the proximal end, i.e., from the functioning of the glands, but from the distal end, i.e., from the psyche, just as if the psyche were itself a substance. For instance, a suitable explanation or a comforting word to the patient can have something like a healing effect, which may even influence the glandular secretions. The doctor's words, to be sure, are 'only' vibrations in the air, yet their special quality is due to a particular psychic state in the doctor. His words are effective only in so far as they convey a meaning or have significance. It is this that makes them work.

But 'meaning' is something mental or spiritual. Call it a

fiction if you like. Nevertheless this fiction enables us to influence the course of the disease far more effectively than we could with chemical preparations. Indeed, we can even influence the bio-chemical processes of the body. Whether the fiction forms itself in me spontaneously or reaches me from outside via human speech, it can make me ill or cure me. Fictions, illusions, opinions are perhaps the most intangible and unreal things we can think of; yet they are the most effective of all in the psychic and even the psychophysical realm.

A psychoneurosis must be understood, ultimately, as the suffering of a soul which has not discovered its meaning. But all creativeness in the realm of the spirit as well as every psychic advance of man arises from the suffering of the soul, and the cause of the suffering is spiritual stagnation, or psychic sterility.

With this realization the doctor sets foot on territory which he enters with the greatest caution. He is now confronted with the necessity of conveying to his patients the healing fiction, the meaning that quickens – for it is this that the sick person longs for, over and above everything that reason and science can give him. He is looking for something that will take possession of him and give meaning and form to the confusion of his neurotic soul . . .

During the past thirty years, people from all the civilized countries of the earth have consulted me. Many hundreds of patients have passed through my hands, the greater number being Protestants, a lesser number Jews, and not more than five or six believing Catholics. Among all my patients in the second half of life – that is to say, over thirty-five – there has not been one whose problem in the last resort was not that of finding a religious outlook on life.

It is safe to say that every one of them fell ill because he had lost what the living religions of every age have given to their followers, and none of them has been really healed who did not regain his religious outlook. This of course has nothing whatever to do with a particular creed or member-ship of a church. ('Psychotherapists or the Clergy', *CW* 11: 490–509)

Jung believed that meaning and 'spirit' can heal psychic illness and even bring relief to physical disease. Before Jung, spiritual meaning was the province of religion and the clergy, but he introduced into medicine the idea that the doctor has a responsibility to bring meaning into a patient's life. Such meaning cannot be imposed on the patient from above, as an act of religious manipulation, but must be discovered with the patient in the context of the therapeutic encounter. The good therapist does not impose, but draws out from the patient what needs to be brought into consciousness.

Jung's discovery of a spiritual factor in healing was probably the last thing medicine wanted to hear. It viewed itself as an exact science and used drugs and chemicals to bring about recovery. As Jung argued, medicine saw itself as a child of nat-ural science, and it shared the same philosophical assumption of material causation. To science, meaning seemed insubstan-tial, ambiguous and elusive. How could such a thing influence the healing of neurosis, much less the organic diseases of the body? The old paradigm assumed that the body was a machine, and that we can understand its working parts in purely chemical and physical terms.

However, the body is connected to the mind, and mind is not reducible to the brain, but is part of the *psyche* (Greek, 'soul'). Jung argued that it is absurd to have a medical psychology without 'psyche', without soul. Much of what takes place in the universities under the name 'psychology' is, according to Jung, a study of human behaviour that has no soul. It is not true psychology because it is a 'logos' without 'psyche'. But just because psyche has no obvious location in the body, no 'place' on a medical chart, is no reason to assume it does not exist. It is a kind of subtle body, an invisible organ of the person, and should be treated as a substance in its own right.

This invisible component of the person requires attention, care and nourishment. Jung borrowed from Catholic theology the idea of the *cura animum*, which advocates care of the soul – in Catholic religion through a relationship with God. The soul is cared for by being recognized. Its form of nourishment is meaning, and meaning arises when the soul feels connected to a larger life. This is wisdom rather than knowledge in the narrow sense, and it is in short supply in the modern world. Nothing is more practical than wise counsel concerning the meaning of life. In states of crisis or emergency, it is only wisdom or insight that is able to pull us through.

Spiritual meaning nourishes the soul by offering it connectedness to a larger life. This gives a sense of identity, and a sense of internal reality and substance. The individual realizes he or she has an 'inner' self and is more than the social mask or persona. This connection to soul is a vital source of health, especially in times of depletion or suffering. People experience soul in different ways; some find it in organized religion, but in the West the majority appear to be post-religious and find soul in personal experiences, the contemplation of nature, the interpretation of dreams and visions, the deepening of human relationships, and personal acts of recognition and awareness.

A key element in the experience of soul is ritual and cere-mony, either organized or impromptu. This can facilitate the sense that there is something 'there' beyond the activities and thoughts of humans. To experience soul is to realize that we are not alone, that intelligent forces interact with our lives and provide meaning and direction if we are receptive to them. In recent times, the best and most accessible study of this subject is Thomas Moore's *Care of the Soul*, a contemporary Jungian reading of the pursuit of soul in everyday life.[32] Jung admitted that connection with soul often comes at the cost of our normal investment in the social persona. To this extent, being normal, he says, is the ideal aim of the unsuccessful (*CW* 10: 511). He recognizes that adaptation to social norms and stereotypes can be fatal to the care of the soul.

Spiritual meaning relates us to each other. A society of strangers only becomes a community through the creation of shared meaning and values. Without this we feel isolated, lonely, cut off. As Marx argued, the primary condition of modern life is alienation, and he prescribed social revolution as the cure. Jung, however, operating with individuals in a clinical setting, prescribed the discovery of meaning as the cure of alienation. Marx adopts the extraverted approach to the regeneration of society and consciousness, and Jung approaches this same aim from the introverted side, seeking renewal through the individuation of the personality.

Jung felt that spirituality was the key to psychic healing. In a famous letter of 1945 he wrote: 'The main interest of my work is not concerned with the treatment of neuroses but rather with the approach to the numinous. But the fact is that the approach to the numinous is the real therapy and inas-much as you attain to numinous experiences you are released from the curse of pathology.'[33] What Jung means by this is that the sense of being connected to something beyond the ego has a healing effect. At the heart of this is a religious theology, a conviction that humanity is made in the image of a sacred other, and that connection with the other is the source of wholeness and renewal. We are not designed to live encapsulated by the ego, but need to see ourselves in relationship with sacred forces.

Jung was a complete relativist at this point. He did not believe that only one source of the holy could have a healing influence. He did not subscribe to the view, for instance, that only Jesus can give us the salvation we need. Jung believed that the numinous could derive from countless sources and religious traditions, from mythologies, cosmologies, esoteric systems, and arts and sciences. Moreover, he believed that the numinous is present, at least potentially, in common experience, and can be felt and made known through meaningful coincidence, synchronicity and an 'inner' relationship with the facts of the world. He did not believe that institutions of faith or creedal doctrines could regulate the spiritual experience, but that such experience occurs spontaneously, as we engage life with depth and commitment.

For Jung, the spiritual is eminently 'natural', it is not supernatural, but 'a deeper dimension of the *real*' (CW 8: 742). By 'real', Jung meant that it exists in some objective and profound sense, but its reality may not be discernible, for instance through reason or logic. Religious institutions, he believed, are arrogant in their belief that the spiritual is somehow dependent on their ministrations or services, and that it comes through them to the people. Institutions are deluded if they adopt this view, but they acquire integrity when they admit they are serving a reality which is greater than themselves, and accessible to all people at all times. Jung was alert to what theologian Paul Tillich called 'religious sin',[34] namely, the misuse of spiritual power by religious institutions, especially if such power is undergirded by fear and guilt.

Jung gave a new angle to the idea of original sin. To him, it was a psychological idea related to our sense of personal alienation from the core of our nature. The ego has 'lapsed' from its pristine origins, and consciousness has been severed from the richness of the unconscious. The overcoming of this sin, for Jung, has nothing to do with being good, or living according to an ethical piety or religious code. It has to do, rather, with seeing beyond the illusion of our separateness and the delusions of ego. In this sense, Jung's ideas are more Eastern than Western. We are 'saved' by glimpses of our true nature, by a psychological enlightenment, and not by an interventionist God, nor by an ethical code. In all of these ideas, one can hear resonances of Jung's philosophical mentors: Nietzsche, Schopenhauer, Goethe, Schiller and William James.

There is ambivalence about the ego in Jung's work. The ego is necessary and essential to life and social adaptation. Without ego, there would be no moral order or social structure. But unless the ego is overcome in ritual, or in moments of transcendence, we exist in a dissociated state which is productive of pathology. As he writes above, the soul is sick when it does not understand its meaning, that is, when it does not feel connected to the soul of the world, the *anima mundi*. Without the experience of transcendence, on a regular basis, the soul becomes sick of itself and tired of the world, because it is 'not of this world', but a fragment of a larger divine nature. In a Platonic gesture, Jung argued that the soul becomes well when it 'remembers' its true belonging. Then it becomes, as Plato argued, *eudaimonic*, full of happiness. Plato believed that remembrance was a core activity of the human soul.

Since the ego resists this belonging, and treats it as some kind of delusion or hoax, the ego is often imagined by Jung as the enemy of health, and the opponent of wholeness. The ego makes a good servant of life, but a lousy master. It has to be criticized and put in its place, especially nowadays, when knowledge and so much that happens in society is used to bolster the ego in its limited view of the world. Thus the ego has to become involved in constant adjustment to the unseen world; it requires 'ongoing conversion' in religious terms, or 'perpetual deconstruction', in philosophical terms.

Spirit inside us longs to unite with spirit in the whole of creation; this is its desire and imperative. Spirit is not content with being an aspect of the personal self, where it is effectively imprisoned, but seeks to be realized on a larger scale. Spirit which is 'caught' in time and space longs to be reunited with spirit in eternity. This sounds grand and pretentious, but it is not as it seems. In ritual and prayer, for instance, we imagine ourselves as participants in a divine drama, as players in a cosmic play. The very word 'ritual' relates to the Latin *ritus*, meaning 'to flow', and this in turn relates to 'river'. In ritual we enter into flow with the universe, and something ancient is released in us at that moment. In this sense, ritual is not in time at all. Its true function is to defeat time and allow us to feel part of eternity.

The spiritual life drives us onward, in search of a fulfilment that appears impossible because it transcends present limits. We exist in time and space and yet we want to make a connection with what is beyond these constrictions. Spirituality initiates what Jung calls the 'symbolic life' (*CW* 18: 627). We feel our lives, in the manner of all symbols, to be pointing towards a greater but hidden reality. The spirit within us 'stands for' something else, and becomes one aspect of a reality whose location is beyond. In the spiritual journey, I realize that I have been fashioned in the image of a reality prior to my existence, and my greatest reward is to find the 'missing piece' that makes my life whole. Indeed, without this missing element, I do not know who I am, since it is only this other who gives me an identity. To live in the spirit is to live this symbolic life, always pointing to something else, in which completion is found.

The word 'symbol' derives from the Greek *symbolon*. It is constituted of the syllable *syn*, meaning 'together', and the word *bolon*, meaning 'to throw'. A symbol is something that has been 'thrown together', comprising a signifier (a word or image) and a less-known signified (a hidden object or refer-ent). The Greeks understood the symbol as a tally, that is, a half of a bone, coin or medal which two parties broke between them to have proof of identity. When fitted together, the two parts of the tally made a whole. We see the same idea today, in friendship necklaces and jewellery tokens that are broken and kept by friends or lovers in remembrance of the other. But the whole idea of friendship and romantic love, in which two parts are brought together to form a whole, is itself symbolic of another level of our experience.

In life, we are signifiers pointing to something unknown. But that unknown reality can become better known, and the spiritual journey is the art of befriending the unknown source which is responsible for our existence. In the state of spiritual health, or psychic wholeness, the self and the ground of its being, its creator, are reunited or 'thrown together'. This deep embrace is often imagined in dreams and fantasies as an erotic conjunction, a sexual union of the human with the divine.

For Jung, as for many mystics in Western and Eastern traditions, sexuality is a symbol of this perpetual human desire to overcome alienation and unite with the heavenly lover in an act of transformation. Much of Jung's writing on alchemy (CW 12, 13, 14) focused on the sexual symbolism of the *coniunctio* or holy marriage (the 'chymical wedding') that represented the achievement of psychospiritual wholeness.

Romantic love evokes the spiritual dimension, because in the image of the beloved we experience the search for the missing piece. This is the archetypal background for such phrases as the 'other half', the 'better half', and related terms that describe the beloved. Our present lives constitute the 'broken off' part that is manifest in time and space. But wherever we go, we point to and carry within ourselves the primordial wholeness which is our ever-present origin.

9

SECULAR SOCIETY AND THE PERILS OF THE SOUL

The unconscious no sooner touches us than we *are* it; we become unconscious of ourselves. That is the age-old danger, instinctively known and feared by primitive man, who himself stands so very close to this pleroma. His consciousness is still uncertain, wobbling on its feet. It is still childish, having just emerged from the primal waters. A wave of the unconscious may easily roll over it, and then he forgets who he was and does things that are strange to him. Hence primitives are afraid of uncontrolled emotions, because consciousness breaks down under them and gives way to possession. All man's strivings have therefore been directed towards the consolidation of consciousness. This was the purpose of rite and dogma; they were dams and walls to keep back the dangers of the unconscious, the 'perils of the soul'. Primitive rites consist accordingly in the exorcizing of spirits, the lifting of spells, the averting of the evil omen, propitiation, purification, and the production by sympathetic magic of helpful occurrences.

It is these barriers, erected in primitive times, that later became the foundations of the Church. It is also these barriers that collapse when the symbols become weak with age. Then the waters rise and boundless catastrophes break over mankind. The religious leader of the Taos pueblo, known as the Loco Tenente Gobernador, once said to me: 'The Americans should stop meddling with our religion, for when it dies and we can no longer help the sun our Father to cross the sky, the Americans and the whole world will learn something in ten years' time, for then the sun won't rise any more.' In other words, night will fall, the light of consciousness is extinguished, and the dark sea of the unconscious breaks in . . .

Since the stars have fallen from heaven and our highest symbols have paled, a secret life holds sway in the unconscious. That is why we have a psychology today, and why we speak of the unconscious. All this would be quite superfluous in an age or culture that possessed symbols. Symbols are spirit from above, and under those conditions the spirit is above too. Therefore it would be a foolish and senseless undertaking for such people to wish to experience or investigate an unconscious that contains nothing but the silent, undisturbed sway of nature. Our unconscious, on the other hand, hides living water, spirit that has become nature, and that is why it is disturbed. Heaven has become for us the cosmic space of the physicists, and the divine empyrean a fair memory of things that once were. But 'the heart glows', and a secret unrest gnaws at the roots of our being. ('Archetypes of the Collective Unconscious', *CW* 9, PART 1: 47–50)

Jung was concerned that modern humanity tries to live without the gods, without a right relationship to the sacred. He feared that we have taken on a condition that is unmanageable, a royal road to ruin. Jung was not a religious spokesman who worried about the moral or ethical condition of people; his concern was with something more basic than ethical standards. It is our psychological health that he was concerned with, our capacity to lose our orientation and become possessed by the powerful forces of the unconscious.

These forces were, he believed, damned up or 'contained' by religion, and when religion is disregarded, the waters of the unconscious crash in, dissolving consciousness and extinguishing the light. Being mindful of the gods is a matter of psychic hygiene, not a matter of piety, social conformity or religiosity.

Secular humanity has got rid of religion because it sees no use for it. It is the enlightenment of the mind that has brought about this desolation. However, in seeking freedom from the gods we find ourselves in the dark, and increasing levels of anxiety and fear constrain us. We have sought the light but have brought darkness upon us, and the hope for a better world to come has eluded us. We must pay the mental and spiritual cost of having no cosmology to contain the forces that have always been perceived as real by our ancestors and their traditions.

Jung often employed the image of a fall: 'the stars have fallen from heaven and our highest symbols have paled'. There are parallels in Jung's work between the condition of the secular West, and the condition of Adam and Eve after the expulsion from the Garden. Both have fallen from a state of grace. Like the First Parents, we are guilty for our actions, for bringing about the collapse of the religious universe: 'To be "unhistorical" is the Promethean sin, and in this sense the modern man is sinful. A higher level of consciousness is like a burden of guilt' (*CW* 10: 152).

Jung believed that modern men and women seek to atone for their guilt by hard work and industry. We are guilty about our nakedness, our squandering of tradition, and we channel this guilt into activity and creativity: 'Modern man must be proficient in the highest degree, for unless he can atone by creative ability for his break with tradition, he is merely disloyal to the past' (*CW* 10: 153). In Jung's view, this may account for the frenetic activity that takes place in the modern world, our desperate, even compulsive attachment to jobs, employment, industry and expansion. We could be atoning for a deep-seated guilt that we cannot articulate.

But we are not just saddled with guilt in secular society. Jung believes that when the gods fall from heaven, when the symbols pale, they don't just go away or disappear. They are reborn, as it were, as turbulent forces in the psyche. When religion collapses, we discover the unconscious and open the Pandora's box of the inner life. 'Our unconscious . . . hides living water, spirit that has become nature, and that is why it is disturbed.' In 'Psychotherapists or the Clergy' he wrote:

It seems to me that, side by side with the decline of religious life, the neuroses grow noticeably more frequent. We are living undeniably in a period of the greatest restlessness, nervous tension, confusion, and disorientation of outlook. (*CW* 11: 514)

His point is that religion is not a mere construction of the rational mind. It is a product of psyche, and of the archetypal realm of the collective unconscious. Since religion has this powerful origin, it cannot be dismissed easily by the mind. We have to face the consequences of the collapse of religion, which are, quite simply, a troubled mind, a disturbed soul.

The forces that were once bound up in religious ritual do not evaporate because we have stopped believing in them. These forces are intrinsic to the human condition and innate to the psyche. They wash back upon us and cause disturbances that we cannot explain. We must remember that Jung was talking about *unconscious* processes in the psyche. Therefore, we cannot be surprised if people do not 'know' about these things. That is why, he believed, we 'need more psychology', so we can regain control of ourselves, get a grasp on our emotions.

Many religious people fail to understand Jung's argument about religion. This is because Jung approached the religious problem through the psychology of the unconscious and religious people approach it through theology. The idea that sacred forces might be responsible for the 'perils of the soul' and increased psychological disorientation conflicts with the notion that God and the sacred are 'good' and cannot wreak havoc upon us. Jung was impatient with this kind of thinking and could not subscribe to it. Jung believed that spirit is a 'mighty daemon', morally neutral or even amoral. To him, the sacred is elemental, vast, ominous and as unpredictable as the forces of nature. It is only we who want the divine to appear 'good'.

The religions, he said, act as 'psychotherapeutic systems' (*CW* 10: 367), as containers of forces that 'attract' our psychic energies, thus freeing us from the necessity of dealing personally with them. When a religion collapses, the energies formerly invested in them flow back into the psyche, and in this process the 'perils of the soul' become a possibility:

> Through his scepticism modern man is thrown back on himself; his energies flow towards their source, and the col-

lision washes to the surface those psychic contents which
are at all times there, but lie hidden in the silt so long as
the stream flows smoothly in its course. (*CW* 10: 162)

When respected in sacred symbols, the archetypes are 'at
rest' and in a stable condition. But when ignored by modernity they become active. Primal forces are 'disturbed' and
have been washed to the surface by our negligence of the
symbolic order. This is, if you will, the 'punishment' inflicted
upon the human soul. We can now see why ancient people
felt the gods punished them when they deserted their cults, or
forgot their oblations. We can begin to understand this
through science, not through superstition. A real strife comes
when we deny the gods. As a result, our present times appear
apocalyptic and dangerous, because the order of the world is
out of balance, and the cosmos and psyche will work to
restore balance, even in the face of our refusal.

Jung's theories help to make new sense of fundamentalist
claims that the world is doomed if we turn away from God.
They are right, in a general way, but in their specific formu-
lations they are hopelessly wrong. The religious fanatic is
indeed in touch with truth, but in such a way that the truth is
distorted, since it is literalized, moralized, and absolutized.

Jung was at pains to explain how internal punishment
works, because it seemed incomprehensible to many people,
especially to scientists. In numerous places he tried to explain
this activity and to help us understand it:

Whenever there is an external form, be it an ideal or a
ritual, by which all the yearnings and hopes of the soul are
adequately expressed, as for instance in a living religion,
then we may say that the psyche is outside and there is no

psychic problem, just as there is then no unconscious in our sense of the word. In consonance with this truth, the discovery of psychology falls entirely within the last decades. (*CW* 10: 159)

We are *homo religiosus* and as such can never depart, for long periods, from our essential nature. In throwing out religion, we have forced ourselves into a critical situation in which mythic forces come to life again within ourselves. They cannot be obliterated, only relocated, because they are fundamental. Before Jung, the philosopher Nietzsche had arrived at exactly the same idea that the soul is activated by the collapse of traditional forms:

All instincts that do not discharge themselves outwardly turn inward – this is what I call the *internalization* of man: thus it was that man first developed what was later called his 'soul'. The entire inner world, originally as thin as if it were stretched between two membranes, expanded and extended itself, acquired depth, breadth, and height, in the same measure as outward discharge was inhibited.[35]

Ironically, the inhibition of religion imposed by the secular order, which ignores the sacred and forgets its presence, serves to activate and intensify the inner life of the soul. Nietzsche's philosophy foreshadowed the discoveries of Jung's psychology.

Analytical psychology has not yet developed an appropriate terminology for this process. Jung refers to it as *introjection*, but it is an odd label in many ways. Introjection does not suggest the magnitude or disastrous impact of this incoming tide. This term would seem to indicate that we are withdrawing 'projections' that belong to the person. However, religious contents were never *personal* in the first place, as they are embedded in a transpersonal field. This problem with terms may reflect a larger problem with psychology. We don't yet know how to talk about subjective processes that are at bottom not subjective at all. The clinical language cannot do justice to this major shift in civilization.

Introjection is a benign euphemism. Psychic disaster might be the more exact term. The mind cannot 'integrate' forces that well up from the depths of religion. It can only wrestle with them, and often succumb to their suggestive power. At best, we can reach a peace with these forces by surrendering to them, or by finding new ways to acknowledge them. Jung famously announced in 1929, 'the Gods have become diseases' (*CW* 13: 54). The diseases that we have exposed ourselves to are not personal, but transpersonal and universal.

In his essays on world events (*CW* 10), Jung was at pains to point out that society is vulnerable to psychic epidemics, since we no longer have any forms to humanize or contain our nonrational impulses. In these essays he argued not only that we can expect an increase in neurotic or mentally disturbed individuals, but that the social fabric itself is disturbed, and increasingly prone to acts of madness, violence and irrationality.

In an interview towards the end of his life, Jung was asked about the state of the world and the character of the next age. He replied:

What comes next? Aquarius, the Waterpourer, the falling of water from one place to another. And the little fish receiving the water from the pitcher . . . But there is danger in the water, on the banks.[36]

There is danger in the water because this is not normal water but supercharged or numinous water. There is 'spirit' in it, and it is restless and hyperactive. As he wrote above: 'Our unconscious hides living water, spirit that has become nature, and that is why it is disturbed.' The psyche registers the influx of archetypal energy as both spiritual and pathological, because we have no public understanding of archetypal forces, which throughout civilization have been known only through the religions.

The idea of psychic inundation is dramatized in countless contemporary films, in which the earth is overwhelmed by enormous waves, hit by asteroids or engulfed by volcanic explosions. These are not only expressions of our physical vulnerability in the universe, but also symbolic expressions of our frailty before the might of the unconscious and its forces. There are as well the more mythological films, in which ancient symbols, objects, legends or gods are awoken from their deep sleep and suddenly activated. Think, for instance, of the movie *Mask*, or of the Indiana Jones series. In the newly aroused state, the ancient symbols bestow enormous yet potentially lethal powers upon those who have activated them.

In his last essay, written in English for a worldwide audience, Jung emphasizes the dire consequences of our lack of awareness of the archetypal forces:

> Our times have demonstrated what it means when the gates of the psychic underworld are thrown open. Things whose enormity nobody could have imagined in the idyllic innocence of the first decade of our century have happened and have turned the world upside down. Ever since, the world has remained in a state of schizophrenia. (*CW* 18: 581)

Jung was the original anti-psychiatrist, who designated society as mad. He was not concerned with repairing broken lives to fit into an insane social order, but had to reverse the directions of psychiatry and argue that society was mad and, as such, individual madness is to be expected as a product of a more general madness.

At this level, a note of alarm and gloom is often found in Jung's writings. Who is able to diagnose and heal the world crisis? Our scientific culture is not shamanic, and cannot give a spiritual response to psychic inundation and flooding. The professions of psychiatry and psychology, for the most part, have no entrance to the numinous, because they have subscribed to a narrow view of personality.

Clergy and ministers might want to help, but generally have no training in depth psychology, and do not relate to the numinous outside its conventional forms. There are important exceptions to the rule, however, especially in American clergy such as Matthew Fox, Morton Kelsey, John Sanford, Sebastian Moore and John Dourley, whose works blend theology and psychology in a new way. They follow Jung in relocating the spiritual forces in the psyche, and showing how theological issues are problems of daily life and not merely found in scripture, history, tradition.

Jung argued that there is no institution or profession that can respond appropriately. There are only individuals, he insisted, from various walks of life, who might be able to see the situation, sense the danger and do something about it. In other words, unusual times call us to be prophetic, to think outside the established structures and the conventional disciplines.

I take heart from the way in which the contemporary arts, music, poetry and film are responding creatively to the spiritual problems of our time. It is the prophetic mode, not the priestly mode, that can find a way through the darkness of our time. And prophecy is the natural domain of the artist. Luke Skywalker trusts the force, but I have come to trust the artist as the intuitive leader of our time.

Jung developed a separate theory about the prophetic nature of the arts (*CW* 15), arguing that the artist expresses the life of the collective unconscious, which contains elements that point to new spiritual possibilities beyond the confusions of society. The spirit of the time (*Zeitgeist*) is found in the arts, but the spirit of religion, Jung felt, is very often dead to the present and speaks mainly to the spirit of the past.

10

PRESENT TENSE, FUTURE TENTATIVE

Now we have no symbolic life, and we are all badly in need of the symbolic life. Only the symbolic life can express the need of the soul – the daily need of the soul, mind you! And because people have no such thing, they can never step out of this mill – this awful, grinding, banal life in which they are 'nothing but'. In religious ritual, however, they are near the Godhead; they are even divine. Think of the priest in the Catholic Church, who is in the Godhead; he carries himself to the sacrifice on the altar; he offers himself as the sacrifice.

Do we do it? Where do we know that we do it? Nowhere! Everything is banal, everything is 'nothing but'; and that is the reason why people are neurotic. They are simply sick of the whole thing, sick of that banal life, and therefore they want sensation. They even want a war; they all want a war. They are all glad when there is a war; they say, 'Thank heaven, now something is going to happen – something bigger than ourselves!'

These things go pretty deep, and no wonder people get neurotic. Life is too rational, there is no symbolic existence in which I am something else, in which I am fulfilling my role, my role as one of the actors in the divine drama of life . . . Then life makes sense, and makes sense in all continuity, and for the whole of humanity. That gives peace, when people feel that they are living the symbolic life, that they are actors in a divine drama. That gives the only meaning to human life; everything else is banal and you can dismiss it. A career, producing children, are all *maya* compared with that one thing, that your life is meaningful.

But . . . we cannot turn the wheel backwards; *we cannot go back* to the symbolism that is gone. Doubt has killed it, has devoured it. So you cannot go back. I cannot go back to the Catholic Church, I cannot experience the miracle of the Mass. I cannot. It is no more true to me; it does not express my psychological condition. My psychological condition wants something else. I must have a situation in which that thing becomes true once more. I need a new form . . . But I am not going to found a religion, and I know nothing about a future religion.

From my observations I learned that the modern unconscious has a tendency to produce a psychological condition which we find, for instance, in medieval mysticism. You find certain things in Meister Eckhart; you find many things in Gnosticism; that is a sort of esoteric Christianity. But Gnosticism is an absolutely consistent development of the idea of Christ within – not the historical Christ without, but the Christ within; and the argument is that it is immoral to allow Christ to suffer for us, that he has suffered enough, and that we should carry our own sins for once and not shift them off on to Christ – that we should carry them all.

That is modern psychology, and . . . that is the future of

which I know – but, of course, the historical future might be quite different . . .

Dreams were the original guidance of man in the great darkness . . . When a man is in the wilderness, the darkness brings the dreams – *somnia a Deo missa* – that guide him. It has always been so. I have not been led by any kind of wisdom; I have been led by dreams, like any primitive. When you are in the darkness you take the next thing, and that is a dream. And you can be sure that the dream is your nearest friend; the dream is the friend of those who are not guided any more by the traditional truth and in consequence are isolated. ('The Symbolic Life', *CW* 18: 627–74)

This is not from a formal essay or piece of writing, but from a recorded conversation between Jung and a group of clergy, bishops and religious people. Jung says we need religion but do not have it. But do we all need religion? Many of us in the secular West would be inclined to say, 'No, Jung, you've got this wrong, I get on very well without it.' Jung would nod and, tapping his pipe, he would say, 'Yes, I understand your point of view.' He would confess that he dislikes formal religion, and has not darkened the doorway of a church for decades.

The problem is one of semantics. By 'religion', Jung means an attitude of reverence towards the whole of life, a sense of the sacred in the everyday, an openness toward the transcendent in self and others. We don't see that as 'religion' because the term has shrunk since Jung's time, to mean something like conventional worship in an institutional setting. Jung is not interested in weekly religious observance, but only in 'the daily need of the soul'. He views the soul as a substance in constant need of reaching beyond itself to a larger life.

We need ecstasy, which in its Greek sense (*ek-stasis*) means to be outside the ego. The ego is a prison, caught in time, space and rationality. We need to leave this mental prison behind from time to time, and on a regular basis. What can get us out? Poetry, love, sex, therapy, passion, nature, ritual, ceremony, music, empathy, compassion, and 'feeling with' the world. All of these things Jung calls 'religion'. Religion is anything that provides escape from egocentricity, relief from the mundane, and as such he gives a Dionysian spin to religion, that seems almost contrary to what an archbishop, for instance, might mean by this term.

In this conversation, Jung speaks about the Aboriginal people of Australia. He makes a vital observation of the Aboriginals based on his reading of anthropological studies of central Australia:

> There is a peculiar value in the symbolic life. It is a fact that the primitive Australians sacrifice to it two-thirds of their available time – of their lifetime in which they are conscious. (*CW* 18: 649)

Today we would refer to 'indigenous' people rather than to 'primitives', but otherwise Jung identified a way of life that recent studies have confirmed. They show that more than half of the waking life of Aboriginals is indeed spent in ritual space, in ceremony and *dadirri* or deep listening to the spirit of things.[37] These studies, however, are speaking of traditional and tribal life, which is disintegrating rapidly in our time. The vacuum created by the loss of ritual life is being replaced by pathology, disease and degeneration, as I have discussed elsewhere.[38]

Aboriginal people were, and some still are, attuned to the

otherness of the world, and Jung condoned this, as it shows an attitude that promotes psychic health. They lived, and some continue to live, in deep connection with the Dreaming, that is, with the layer of experience that Jung would call the 'collective unconscious', or what the poet Yeats, for instance, would call the *spiritus mundi* or world spirit. However, if such people are deprived of their relationship to the Dreaming, through colonization, alienation from tribal lands and practices, a traumatic reaction ensues. Colonial governments offer money and token support, but the soul has been injured by experiences that are catastrophic and often irreversible.

Deprived of ritual space, ceremony and opportunities for *ek-stasis*, many indigenous people lose their orientation and health. They fall prey to mental illness, personality disorder, depression and anxiety, self-destructive behaviours, glue sniffing or 'chroming', crime, violence and suicide.[39] What we see in the tragedy of such indigenous peoples, not only in Australia but in the United States, Canada, Mexico, Africa, and wherever colonization has inflicted its violence and disruption, is symbolic of what is happening in the Western European psyche at the same time. When rationality takes over, when greed destroys cultural values, when mind triumphs over the subtle levels of existence, the soul suffers and perishes.

When First World people look at drunken indigenous Fourth World people and shake their heads in disapproval, they are looking into the depths of their own souls, feeling uneasy about the disease that has already afflicted them from the inside. It is simply that the indigenous people have less to fall back on, less material culture and affluence to absorb the shock that comes from the condition that shamanic cultures call *loss of soul*. Jung saw this as not just a colourful phrase or fancy term. It is a real condition, found wherever the means of transcendence is abolished by progress. When transcendence is lost, we fall more readily into the forces that lead to degeneration. Or, in the words of scripture, 'When there is no vision, the people perish' (Proverbs 29: 18).

Jung said we have no symbolic life and are in need of it. He claimed we cannot stand 'this awful, grinding, banal life' and will do anything to escape it. We create the banality by refusing transcendence, and then we are forced to invent escape routes. Any form of sensation will do. He said we invent fads and fashions to break out of our banality: new kinds of music, dance, travel, sport, entertainment, appliances, gadgets, technologies (CW 10: 488F). We become 'hooked' on common forms of sensation and novelty, and the profit-making industries understand our obsessions and are happy to cater to them.

However, since the psyche is predisposed to transcendence, such experiences often happen quite spontaneously and unconsciously. Jung saw neurosis and mental illness as negative forms of transcendence. Hence 'no wonder people get neurotic', because without deliberate avenues for transcendence the only expressions available are negative and destructive.

Jung lived through two world wars, and wrote several essays on the love of war. He felt that war is one of society's favoured forms of negative transcendence. When people say they 'need' a war, they are saying they need to break out of the prison-house of reason, and indulge a bout of unreason, usually at the expense of another people, nation or race. The attraction of war is that the negative forces building up in the psyche are felt to be the other person's fault. It is easier to deal with negativity if it is projected outside and made a political problem with one's neighbour.

For Jung, 'they are all glad when there is a war', because it is a ritualistic rip-up of our rationality and a release of energies which have become impossible to contain by normal means. We will always lurch from one devastating explosion to another, from criminality to genocidal impulses, because there is so much irrationality that demands release and cannot be expressed.

Our rationality is in one sense a crowning achievement of the ages and a prize of evolution. We have to nurture it and not allow it to be overthrown by disintegrative forces. But Jung's belief was that if we cling too tightly to rationality, it is overthrown by forces that cannot be humanized. We have to find the courage to hand some of our rationality back to the gods, in ritual and ceremony. When we sacrifice some of our rationality, in a state of reverence, we are made more human, because we have recognized that forces move through us that belong to the cosmos. That frees us from being possessed by these forces and we can return to our human form.

Either we sacrifice some of our rationality for the sake of growth, or we are sacrificed, savagely and brutally, to growth gone wrong. This is an urgent message of his psychology, and a theme that preoccupied Jung to his last days. It is a message that is easy to distort, sensationalize and misinterpret, as has been the case recently.[40]

How do we recover our symbolic or nonrational life? Jung is not too clear on this point. He is tentative, with a few suggestions. He was tempted to support a renewal of Christianity, and in particular Roman Catholicism, which has a richer symbolic life than the more modern and intellectual Protestant tradition. At one point, Jung even received a blessing from Pope Pius XII, in recognition of his achievement of returning 'certain important Catholics' to the community of the faithful (*CW* 18: 618). Jung said that people who had lapsed from their natal faith ought to return to their tradition before journeying to the East, or to esotericisms of the ancient past.

But contradictions abound: Jung makes it clear in this extract that he 'cannot go back' to the Roman Church, much as he might like to. It is not an option. That symbolic form cannot 'work' for him any more. It has been seen through by reason, 'doubt has killed it, has devoured it . . . so you cannot go back'. Why did he send others back, then? One answer is that he was a radical pluralist, and what suited him personally was not imposed on anyone else. Jung was more concerned about the need to find a symbolic life than he was about what kind of symbolic life.

However, Jung was insistent that a return to Christian *fundamentalism* is out of the question for modernity. We cannot embrace it, for it belongs to a stage of literal thinking that the West has outgrown. When Jung sent people back, he hoped they would find a new relation to faith. He hoped they would read the dogmas symbolically and not literally, viewing ritual and ceremony through the eyes of a poet. Scientific humanity can no longer believe literally in transubstantiation (the changing of the bread and wine into the body and blood of Christ), an idea that was no longer tenable even in the fifteenth century, at the time of Martin Luther. At that stage, the Protestant Reformation changed the literal transformation of the mass into a symbolic gesture, and Jung was very much a Protestant on this point.

If we are to find a symbolic life today, it cannot contradict reason in the manner of Christian doctrine, or appear absurd to the mind, as do the dogmas of the Virgin Birth and the Physical Resurrection. A truly modern symbolic life will have to include reason within itself, and perhaps transcend reason in a movement towards mystery and unknowable reality. But to oppose faith and reason in the traditional manner is disastrous, and one reason why, according to Jung, Christianity in its old form is now a wineskin that is beyond patching (CW 9, 1: 1f).

Jung believed that the collapse of Western Christianity has left us in a very primitive place. We exist in dark times, and the guiding lights of revelation have deserted us, because we can no longer believe in them. Jung suggested two possible ways forward: one is to rework the entire religious tradition, reading everything in a symbolic light, as metaphor, and not as history or fact. He often said that the task ahead for Christianity is to find the courage to deconstruct itself, and to downgrade all of its dogmas from metaphysical facts to metaphorical fictions (CW 11).

It is hardly likely that the Vatican or Canterbury will follow this lead, although some theologians and philosophers are trying to reconstruct religion along poetic and metaphorical lines. There is a progressive theological discourse that attempts to convert metaphysics into metaphor, and dogma into symbolic process.[41] What Jung called for seventy years ago is today being discovered as a possible way forward for post-metaphysical theology and postmodern philosophy.

It is difficult, however, to uproot a tradition from literal thinking and to reconstruct it as poetry and symbolic discourse. The difficulty takes us back to the problem of reality: if something did not happen as fact or history, can it still be regarded as real and true? Jung would say, 'Yes, it is psychologically true and symbolically real.' This is not likely to appeal to most Western 'believers' who want something to be historically factual before it can be believed. Jung would simply say that such believers have no imagination and, as such, are forced to fabricate an unreal history in which 'supernatural' or miraculous events are claimed to have occurred.

Apart from turning to the East, which he did not readily condone, the other way for Westerners to move, according to Jung, is towards personal dreams and intuition. Here Jung anticipated the postmodern concern for the art of the small and individual meaning-making after the collapse of the great narratives of Western Christianity. 'Dreams were the original guidance of man in the great darkness', and Jung assumed that we are in great darkness again, since the light of revelation has been extinguished. If the light of religion can be imagined as the bright light of the sun, the light of dreams and intuitions is like the starry firmament. We have lost the dominant solar blaze, and walk around in near darkness, but what we have within our grasp are the little lights, the splinters or flints of light, that we get from dreams, hunches, visions or meaning-ful occurrences in the day.

These are fairly modest and small, to be sure, but Jung insisted they are reliable, and all we have in a world where sus-picion and doubt has killed off the sources of light. Jung once asked a Jesuit father about his view regarding dreams, and the priest said, 'Well, there we have to be careful, and we are already a bit suspect. We [the clergy] have the means of grace of the Church.' The Jesuit is saying that the grace of the Church should prevail over any 'superstitious' concern for dreams, which looks 'suspect' to formal religious tradition. Jung's response to the priest is significant:

Right you are, you don't need dreams. I can give no abso-lution, I have no means of grace; therefore I must listen to dreams. I am a primitive; you are a civilized man. I cannot

be a saint – I can only be . . . very primitive, going by the
next thing, quite superstitious. (*CW* 18: 682)

The times have returned us to an earlier age. It is as if we
now scratch around in the sand, whereas before we painted
glorious canvases to gods and saints whose lives we knew and
in whom we believed. The movement from religion to psychology is paralleled by similar developments in the arts over
the modern period: from a world of settled and grand forms,
beautifully delineated by a masterly craft, to humbler, broken,
fragmented forms such as we find in Picasso, Braque, Joyce,
Eliot, Cage or Stravinsky.

Although it is always tempting to go back to the glory days
of the past, we have to be true to the present, true to discord
and brokenness, and find value and truth in the little revela-
tions that are afforded us in dreams, intuitions, artworks,
movies, love songs. This is the postmodern condition, but
Jung described it a long while before postmodernism was
invented.

Jung believed that the art of the small reveals the big.
Hence his constant reference to the link between our time
and 'medieval mysticism'. There is a meaning in the inward
turn of our time, the turn towards psyche and interiority. It is
not just about narcissism or selfishness, but about realizing
the greatness within the human, and the vastness within the
soul. This must not inflate our importance, however, because
we are to see ourselves as carriers of forces that transcend us.
When we achieve that perspective, Jung argued, we will
return to sanity in our culture and in our selves.

NOTES

1 See for instance, the study on the post-secular condition of postmodern society, in John Caputo, *On Religion* (London: Routledge, 2001); and a similar account found in Peter Berger, *The Desecularization of the World* (Grand Rapids: Eerdmans, 1999).

2 Freud, in a letter of 1908 to Karl Abraham of Berlin, quoted in Paul Stepansky, 'Jung, Freud and the Burdens of Discipleship', in Renos Papadopoulos (ed.), *Carl Gustav Jung: Critical Assessments* (London: Routledge, 1992), p. 191.

3 Freud, in a letter to Jung, 16 April 1909, in William McGuire (ed.), *The Freud/Jung Letters* (Princeton University Press, 1974), p. 218.

4 See for instance, Joseph Chilton Pearce, *The Biology of Transcendence* (Rochester: Park Street Press, 2002); Gregg Jacobs, *The Ancestral Mind* (New York: Viking, 2003); Joel Kovel, *History and Spirit* (Boston: Beacon Press, 1991).

5 A popular introduction to the 'Jungian' turn in postmodern science is found in Fritjof Capra, *The Turning Point: Science, Society and the Rising Culture* (London: Flamingo, 1982).

6 See David Tracy, *On Naming the Present* (London: SCM Press, 1994). See also Christine Gallant, *Tabooed Jung: Marginality as Power* (New York University Press, 1996).

7 References to the *Collected Works* of Jung are denoted throughout this book in parentheses by *CW*, followed by the relevant volume and paragraph numbers. Please note it is standard practice to refer to the paragraph, not to the page number, of Jung's writings. Referencing is omitted where the citation is from the chosen extract. The full bibliographical reference is: Jung, C. G. 1953–83: *The Collected Works of C. G. Jung*, translated by R. F. C. Hull, edited by Sir Herbert Read, Michael Fordham, Gerhard Adler and

William McGuire, published in England by Routledge and in the United States by Princeton University Press, Bollingen Series XX. There are twenty volumes in the collected works, plus four supplementary volumes.

8   This work went through several editions and changes of title. Its original German title was *Wandlungen und Symbole der Libido* (1912), and it was first named in English, *Psychology of the Unconscious* (1916). We know the book today as *Symbols of Transformation*, after Jung's fourth and greatly revised edition of 1952.

9   This view of Jung's is identical to that of the philosopher Hegel; see Frederick G. Weiss (ed.), *Hegel: The Essential Writings* (New York: Harper & Row, 1974).

10   Walter A. Shelburne, *Mythos and Logos in the Thought of Carl Jung* (Albany: State University of New York Press, 1988).

11   Richard Noll, *The Jung Cult: Origins of a Charismatic Movement* (Princeton University Press, 1994); and Richard Noll, *The Aryan Christ: The Secret Life of Carl Jung* (New York: Random House, 1997).

12   Sonu Shamdasani, *Cult Fictions: C. G. Jung and the Founding of Analytical Psychology* (London and New York: Routledge, 1998).

13   See James Hillman's works listed in Suggestions for Further Reading.

14   A. D. Hope, 'An Epistle from Holofernes' (1960), in *Selected Poems* (Sydney: Angus & Robertson, 1992), p. 56.

15   Jung, *Memories, Dreams, Reflections* (1961) (New York: Random House, 1995). There is much discussion about whether this should be referred to as an 'autobiography'. The current view in Jung scholarship is that *MDR* should be seen as a biography written by Jung's secretary, Aniela Jaffé, in which Jung contributed some important passages.

16   Jung, 'The *Face to Face* Interview' (1959), in William McGuire and R. F. C. Hull (eds.), *C. G. Jung Speaking* (London: Picador, 1980), p. 383.

17   Because of Aboriginal sensitivity to gender, and to the separation of men's and women's business, I am unable to comment on women's business. For more on tribal initiation, see my 'Rites and Wrongs of Passage', in *Remaking Men* (London and New York: Routledge, 1997).

18 Cited by Erich Neumann, in his *The Origins and History of Consciousness* (1949) (Princeton University Press, 1973), p. 289.

19 See Keith Ansell Pearson, *How to Read Nietzsche* (London: Granta Books, 2005), p. 30ff.

20 This idea was first suggested by Marie-Louise von Franz, 'The Underground God', in her *C. G. Jung: His Myth in Our Time* (Boston: Little, Brown, 1975), p. 29ff.

21 Jung confessed to Freud that as a boy he had been 'the victim of a sexual assault' by a man he once 'worshipped'; see *The Freud/Jung Letters*, ed. William McGuire (Princeton University Press, 1974), 49J, 95.

22 Victor White, *God and the Unconscious* (1952) (Dallas: Spring Publications, 1982).

23 This relationship is sensitively traced in Deirdre Bair, *Jung: A Biography* (London: Little, Brown, 2004).

24 David Tacey, *The Spirituality Revolution: The Emergence of Contemporary Spirituality* (London and New York: Routledge, 2004).

25 Robert Johnson, *Owning Your Own Shadow: Understanding the Dark Side of the Psyche* (HarperSanFrancisco, 1993).

26 Philip Rieff, *The Triumph of the Therapeutic* (New York: Harper & Row, 1966).

27 W. B. Yeats, 'The Second Coming', in Timothy Webb (ed.), *W. B. Yeats: Selected Poetry* (Harmondsworth: Penguin, 1991), p. 124.

28 See for instance Robert Bly, *Iron John: A Book About Men* (Reading, Mass.: Addison-Wesley, 1990); Jean Shinoda Bolen, *Goddesses in Everywoman* (New York: Harper Collophon, 1985); and Robert Moore and Douglas Gillette, *King, Warrior, Magician, Lover* (San Francisco: HarperCollins, 1990).

29 James Hillman, *The Myth of Analysis* (New York: Harper & Row, 1972), p.50.

30 Andrew Samuels, *The Political Psyche* (London: Routledge, 1993); Susan Rowland, *Jung: A Feminist Revision* (Cambridge: Polity, 2001); Demaris Wehr, *Jung and Feminism: Liberating Archetypes* (Boston: Beacon Press, 1987); Sue Austin, *Women's Aggressive Fantasies* (London: Brunner-Routledge, 2005).

31 Donald Kalsched, *The Inner World of Trauma: Archetypal Defenses of the Personal Spirit* (London and New York: Brunner-Routledge, 1996).

32 Thomas Moore, *Care of the Soul* (New York: Harper Collins, 1992).

33 Jung, in a 1945 letter to P. W. Martin, in *C. G. Jung Letters*, selected and edited by Gerhard Adler, translated by R. F .C. Hull, Vol. 1, (Princeton University Press, 1973), p. 377.

34 Paul Tillich, *The Shaking of the Foundations* (Harmondsworth: Penguin, 1949).

35 Friedrich Nietzsche, *The Genealogy of Morals*, trans. W. Kaufmann (New York: Random House, 1989), pp. 84–5.

36 Jung, 'On the frontiers of knowledge' (1959), in William McGuire and R. F. C. Hull (eds.), *C. G. Jung Speaking* (London: Picador, 1980), pp. 370–2.

37 Eugene Stockton, *The Aboriginal Gift: Spirituality for a Nation* (Sydney: Millennium Books, 1995).

38 David Tacey, *Edge of the Sacred* (Sydney: HarperCollins, 1995).

39 Craig San Roque, 'A long weekend in Alice Springs, Central Australia', in Thomas Singer and Samuel L. Kimbles, *The Cultural Complex: Contemporary Jungian Perspectives on Psyche and Society* (Hove and New York: Brunner-Routledge, 2004).

40 Richard Wolin, *The Seduction of Unreason: from Nietzsche to Postmodernism* (Princeton University Press, 2004).

41 Mark Wrathnall, *Religion After Metaphysics* (Cambridge University Press, 2003); and Graham Ward, ed., *The Postmodern God* (Oxford: Blackwell, 1997).

CHRONOLOGY

1875 Born on 26 July in Kesswil, Switzerland to Paul and Emilie Jung.

1895–1900 Medical training and qualification at Basel University.

1896 Death of father.

1900–1909 Works under Eugen Bleuler at the Burghölzli, the insane asylum of psychiatric clinic of Zurich University.

1903 Marriage to Emma Rauschenbach; one son and four daughters.

1905–13 Appointed *Privatdozent* (lecturer) on the medical faculty of Zurich University; lectures on psychoneuroses and psychology.

1906 Correspondence with Freud begins.

1907 First meeting with Freud in Vienna.

1909 Withdraws from the clinic to devote himself to private practice; first visit to the USA, with Freud and Ferenczi; moves to his own house in Küsnacht/Zurich.

1910–14 First president of the International Psychoanalytic Association.

1912 Publishes *Wandlungen und Symbole der Libido* (*Psychology of the Unconscious*, 1916) leading to:

1913 Break with Freud; designates his psychology 'Analytical Psychology'; resigns lectureship at Zurich University.

1913–19 Period of great psychic disorientation, his 'confrontation with the unconscious'.

1921 Publishes *Psychological Types*; first use of term 'Self'.

1923 Builds tower in Bollingen; death of mother; association begins with Richard Wilhelm.

1924–5 Trip to the USA; visits Pueblo Indians in New Mexico.

1925–6 Expedition to Kenya, Uganda and the Nile; visit with the Elgonyi on Mount Elgon.

1928 Begins study of alchemy; *Two Essays on Analytical Psychology*.

1933 Lectures at the Eidgenössische Technische Hochschule (ETH),

Zurich (Swiss Federal Polytechnic) on modern psychology; publishes *Modern Man in Search of a Soul*.

1934 Founds International General Medical Society for Psychotherapy and becomes its first president.

1934–9 Seminar series on psychological aspects of Nietzsche's *Zarathustra*.

1935 Appointed titular professor at the ETH, Zurich; lectures at the Tavistock, London.

1936 Receives honorary doctoral degree from Harvard University.

1937 Terry Lectures on 'Psychology and Religion' at Yale University.

1941 Publishes, together with Karl Kerényi, *Essays on a Science of Mythology*.

1944 Publishes *Psychology and Alchemy*.

1948 Inauguration of the C. G. Jung Institute, Zurich.

1951–2 Publishes *Aion*; *Symbols of Transformation* (greatly revised edition of *Psychology of the Unconscious*), 'Answer to Job'; together with Wolfgang Pauli, 'Synchronicity'.

1953 Publication commences of the *Collected Works* (translated by R. F. C. Hull).

1955 Death of his wife; honorary doctorate of the ETH, on the occasion of his eightieth birthday.

1955–6 *Mysterium Coniunctionis*, his final and classic work on alchemy.

1957 Starts work on *Memories, Dreams, Reflections*, in collaboration with Aniela Jaffé.

1961 Completes *Man and His Symbols*; dies on 6 June in Küsnacht/Zurich.

SUGGESTIONS FOR FURTHER READING

By Jung

Jung is the best introduction to his own work, and the most accessible writings include:

Memories, Dreams, Reflections (1961) (New York: Random House, 1995).

Modern Man in Search of a Soul (1933) (London and New York: Routledge Classics, 2004).

On the Nature of the Psyche (1947/1954) (London and New York: Routledge Classics, 2002).

Two Essays on Analytical Psychology (1953/1966), Vol. 7 of the *Collected Works*, 1972.

Readers

C. G. Jung: Psychological Reflections, selected and edited by Jolande Jacobi (New Jersey: Princeton University Press, 1970).

The Essential Jung: Selected Writings, selected and introduced by Anthony Storr (London: Fontana Press, 1983).

The Portable Jung, edited by Joseph Campbell (Harmondsworth: Penguin, 1976).

Jung's Life

Deirdre Bair, *Jung: A Biography* (London: Little, Brown, 2004).

Frank McLynn, *Carl Gustav Jung* (London: Bantam Press, 1996).

Gerhard Wehr, *Jung: A Biography* (Boston: Shambhala, 1987).

General Overviews

Ann Casement, *Carl Gustav Jung* (London: Sage Publications, 2001).

C. G. Jung, ed., *Man and His Symbols* (London: Aldus Books, 1964).

June Singer, *Boundaries of the Soul* (New York: Doubleday, 1972).

Murray Stein, *Jung's Map of the Soul: An Introduction* (Chicago: Open Court, 1998).

Anthony Stevens, *On Jung* (London: Penguin, 1999).

Marie-Louise von Franz, *C. G. Jung: His Myth in Our Time* (New York: G. P. Putnam's, 1975).

Edward C. Whitmont, *The Symbolic Quest* (New Jersey: Princeton University Press, 1991).

Polly Young-Eisendrath and Terence Dawson, *The Cambridge Companion to Jung* (Cambridge: Cambridge University Press, 1997).

Intellectual Context

Paul Bishop, *Jung in Contexts: A Reader* (London and New York: Routledge, 1999).

J. J. Clarke, *In Search of Jung* (London and New York: Routledge, 1992).

Henri Ellenberger, *The Discovery of the Unconscious* (New York: Basic Books, 1970).

George Hogenson, *Jung's Struggle with Freud* (Wilmette: Chiron Publications, 1994).

John Kerr, *A Most Dangerous Method* (New York: Knopf, 1993).

Histories of Analytical Psychology

Thomas Kirsch, *The Jungians* (London: Routledge, 2000).

Sonu Shamdasani, *Jung and the Making of Modern Psychology: The Dream of a Science* (Cambridge: Cambridge University Press, 2003).

Analytical Psychology After Jung

Michael Vannoy Adams, *The Mythological Unconscious* (London and New York: Karnac, 2001).

Ann Casement, ed., *The Post-Jungians Today* (London and New York: Routledge, 1998).

James Hillman, *The Myth of Analysis* (Evanston: Northwestern University Press, 1972).

James Hillman, *Re-Visioning Psychology* (New York: Harper and Row, 1975).

Susan Rowland, *Jung: A Feminist Revision* (Cambridge: Polity, 2002).

Andrew Samuels, *Jung and the Post-Jungians* (London: Routledge, 1985).

David Tacey, *Remaking Men: Jung, Spirituality and Social Change* (London and New York: Routledge, 1997).

Applying Jung

Karin Barnaby and Pellegrino d'Acierno, eds., *C. G. Jung and the Humanities* (New Jersey: Princeton University Press, 1990).

Roger Brooke, *Jung and Phenomenology* (London and New York: Routledge, 1990).

J. J. Clarke, *Jung and Eastern Thought* (London and New York: Routledge, 1994).

Christopher Hauke, *Jung and the Postmodern* (London and Philadelphia: Routledge, 2000).

Lucy Huskinson, *Nietzsche and Jung: The Whole Self in the Union of Opposites* (Hove and New York: Brunner-Routledge, 2004).

Andrew Samuels, *The Political Psyche* (London and New York: Routledge, 1993).

David Tacey, *Jung and the New Age* (Hove and Philadelphia: Brunner-Routledge, 2001).

Web Resources

http://www.jungianstudies.org/ Website of the International Association for Jungian Studies http://www.iaap.org/ Website of the International Association for Analytical Psychology

http://www.cgjungpage.org/ Website for C. G. Jung, Analytical Psychology and Culture

INDEX

14 Jung's method of dream interpretation is not association, but amplification — relating symbols to archetypes of history, mythology, and world religions, a broad perspective not a personal perspective

17 The importance of art & symbolic language to the ego

18 The psychological forces of healing cannot be known as rational concepts, but only as poetic symbols

19 Ego fears the Mother because it may be trapped in the deep unconscious; Liesl seems more like the mother than the shadow

21 Anima is a function of relationship with ego after some individuation

67 Young males emotionally attached to their mothers need social initiation rites to create separation and to claim their masculinity

76 Alchemy compared to psychotherapy

87 Spiritual dimension of healing; finding soul in personal experiences, in visions, dreams
ie. Dunstan's vision of Mrs. Dempster

90 Ego must be overcome in ritual & experience transcendence.

92-93 Sexual union of human & divine: perpetual human desire to overcome alienation; Chymical marriage represents psycho-spiritual wholeness
Mary Dempster was a physical embodiment of this for the tramp.